Creation

In the Beginning and Afterward

Arthur A. Eggert

In Terra Pax Lutheran Publishing

Sun Prairie, Wisconsin

Cover photograph: Green Bay, Wisconsin

                        Photograph by Joan Eggert

All Scripture quotations, unless otherwise indicated, have been taken from the Evangelical Heritage Version®, copyright © 2018 by the Wartburg Project. Used by permission. Evangelical Heritage Version® is a federally registered trademark of the Wartburg Project.

Copyright © 2022 by In Terra Pax Lutheran Publishing. All rights reserved. No part of this publication may be reproduced, stored in a retrieval system, or transmitted in any form or by any means–electronic, mechanical, photocopy, recording, or otherwise–except for brief quotations in reviews, without prior permission from the publisher. For permissions, write: In Terra Pax, 994 Hunters Trail, Sun Prairie, WI 53590.

ISBN: 979-8-98-587150-0

Library of Congress Control Number: 2022904218

Table of Contents

	Introduction	1
Chapter 1	The Creator	5
Chapter 2	From Eternity	15
Chapter 3	In the Beginning	23
Chapter 4	Populating the Creation	35
Chapter 5	Continuing Revelation on the Creation	51
Chapter 6	Man - God's Special Creature	61
Chapter 7	Preservation – God's Continuing Work of Creation	73
Chapter 8	God's Re-Creation of Man	87
Chapter 9	Judgment - The End of the Creation	101
Chapter 10	Creation and the Lutheran Confessions	107
Chapter 11	Science and Theology	119
Chapter 12	Creation Apologetics	133
Chapter 13	Flawed Apologetic Approaches	149
	Conclusion	161
	Bibliography	163
	Index	165

The Author

Arthur Eggert has an extensive background in the physical and cognitive sciences. He received a PhD from the University of Wisconsin-Madison in analytical chemistry and has taught chemistry at Duke University. For 41 years he was a tenure-track professor in the Department of Pathology and Laboratory Medicine at the UW-Madison and its Medical School. Dr. Eggert served as the director of informatics for the clinical laboratories of the affiliated university hospital, eventually becoming the chief of the hospital's clinical pathology service and the administrative director of its clinical laboratories. His research included the design of computer hardware and software, the flow of laboratory specimens and information in a medical environment, the chemistry teaching program called CHEMPROF, and the human-computer interface.

Dr. Eggert has taught biblical doctrine and church history classes in WELS churches in the Madison area for more than 30 years. He has served on the Self-Study Committee for WELS Ministerial Training Schools, the Western Wisconsin District Commission on Adult Discipleship, and the Wisconsin Lutheran Seminary Governing Board. He currently is a member of the WELS Institute for Lutheran Apologetics. He is the author of numerous articles that have appeared in *Forward in Christ*, *What About Jesus*, and the *Wisconsin Lutheran Quarterly* and has presented three pastoral conference papers. He is the author of *Simply Lutheran* (Northwestern Publishing House), a resource to strengthen the doctrinal understanding of Lutheran laypeople; author of *Christian, Lutheran, Confessional* (In Terra Pax Lutheran Publishing), a book on church history; and a co-author of *Clearing a Path for the Gospel* (In Terra Pax Lutheran Publishing), a book on Lutheran apologetics.

Reviewers and Commentators

The author wishes to thank the following people who read all or part of this manuscript and made useful theological, technical, and structural comments that enhanced its quality.

Rev. Shaun Arndt, WELS,
    Parish pastor
Dr. Paul Boehlke, WELS
    Emeritus biology professor, Wisconsin Lutheran College
Joan Eggert, WELS
    Clinical laboratory scientist (retired)
Katerina Eggert, WELS
    High school junior
Sharon Grinyer, WELS
    Insurance claims adjustor (retired)
Patricia Horstmeier, ELS
    Clinical laboratory scientist (retired)
Jane Kohlwey, WELS
    Attorney (retired)
Emily Mandler, WELS
    Agronomist
Bonnie Schmidt, LCMS
    High school teacher (retired)
Rev. Scott Schwertfeger, WELS
    Parish Pastor
Rev. Daniel Sims, WELS
    Director of Christian Aid and Relief
Rev. Dr. Bill Tackmier, WELS
    Professor, Wisconsin Lutheran Seminary
Sally Wellman, ELS
    Attorney (retired)

Introduction

When we look around us in the world, we observe objects of various types. Some are natural and some are manmade. Some are old and some are new. We are often curious about these objects and want to learn more about them, including who invented them or who manufactured them. We might be curious about whether they come in different sizes or colors. Concerning people, we might be interested in where they or their ancestors came from. Considering ourselves, we might be interested in our own ancestors and might even do genealogical research to learn more about ourselves.

When it comes to the objects of nature, we may have questions about how things grow and how things that appear similar are related to each other. Some people are interested in improving the breeds of certain animals, such as dogs or cows. Some look at what might be done to create healthier and more pest-resistant plants. Because all manmade objects had a creator, it is natural to ask whether the natural things we see around us also had a creator or whether they somehow developed from simpler materials. Some people even want to know how humans came about or, more existentially, why we exist. We can, indeed, generate many questions about ourselves and the things around us—some of great significance and others of mere curiosity. In this book we will explore where we came from and why we are here in the light of God's revelation.

Through the Scriptures, i.e., the Bible, the LORD[1] has revealed the truths he wants people to know about his actions and plans. He has not divulged everything that we might desire to know, nor has he arranged his teachings using a detailed syllabus as a professor might in presenting a college course. This apparently unsystematic presentation in the Bible resulted from God's revealing information over time as it was needed by the people God had called to be his followers. Gradually, he revealed more and more of his message for humanity until he had given us all that we need to know about him, about the

---

[1] "The LORD" is the name of the almighty God described in the Bible.

physical universe he had created, and about his plan of salvation for fallen mankind.

In studying revelation given by the LORD, it is useful for us to group all the information on each specific teaching, i.e., on an individual doctrine, so we can understand what God wants to communicate more accurately than we could if we read only isolated verses or sections of Scripture. We frequently work in much the same manner when we try to fully understand the intent of a human author or speaker. We seek to hear or to read the person's ideas in more than one context to fully grasp what that person wants to convey to us. For famous people, such as Martin Luther,[2] we might find whole books concerning their views on a specific topic.

Creation is a topic on which a considerable amount of material exists in the Bible, and creation is both the title and the subject of this book. In the biblical presentation of doctrines, however, they are often interleafed with other material because God revealed them in a manner so they could be understood by their first readers and hearers. Therefore, sometimes it is necessary to discuss related themes in addition to the central topic being considered. For this purpose, Concordia Publishing House provides a volume called *A Summary of Christian Doctrine*,[3] and Northwestern Publishing House has produced a collection of books entitled the People's Bible Teaching series. Each of these assembles the information from the Scriptures by doctrine, so its readers can learn how the whole counsel of God's Word relates to the individual teachings. To the extent he can, the author will refer to these CPH and NPH books to avoid rewriting what their authors have already clearly presented. Notwithstanding this, the author will cover relevant points in sufficient detail when they bear on the topic of creation, so the reader does not continually need to reference other volumes.

Creation is always a topic of great interest because it contains ideas that numerous people find hard to accept, difficult to comprehend, or even emotionally unsettling. In writing about creation, some authors have attacked it as unscientific, while other authors have attacked scientific practices. Some authors have tried to defend the biblical account by overstating what the Bible really says or by altering the meaning of the text for strategic advantage. Authors have even become polemic in their attacks or defenses of the biblical ac-

---

[2] Dr. Martin Luther was a sixteenth century Augustinian monk whose posting of 95 debate propositions in 1517 sparked the Protestant Reformation.

[3] Edward W. A. Koehler, *A Summary of Christian Doctrine*, 3rd, Brent W. Kuhlman, ed. (Saint Louis: Concordia Publishing House, 2006).

count, implying that believers or unbelievers are either blatantly dishonest or foolish. This book is not written in any of these manners. It presents what the Bible clearly says about creation—no more and no less.[4] It discusses the "real world" implications of God's actions, as well as honestly contrasting what the biblical account says with what scientists have learned from their studies and with what others have concluded based on their assumptions.

The author has written this book with a firm belief in *sola scriptura*, in the sufficiency of the Scriptures, and in the principle that Scripture must interpret Scripture, rather than Scripture being interpreted by reason, by the teaching authorities of any church body, or based on scientific models.

Arthur Eggert, 2022

---

[4] Do not add to the word that I am commanding you, and do not subtract from it, so that you keep the commandments of the Lord your God that I am commanding you. (Deuteronomy 4:2)

1

The Creator

The universe and the God who created it are entities beyond our ability to completely understand. Yet, if we are not to simply stand around with our mouths open in wonder about them or to ignore them as something about which we need not concern ourselves, then we must set the stage and bring the central, in fact, the only, actor out upon it. After that, we can begin to explore what God the Creator has done.

The "Creations" of Man

As people look up from their place of work or play, often everything they see in their vicinity was human-created and human-produced. Unless they have a window through which they can peer into the natural world, every item around them, whether in the office, in the kitchen, in the shop, or in the gymnasium, was developed through human ingenuity and human manufacturing skill. Most of us live our lives in environments that are almost entirely controlled by human inventions. The illumination by which we work, the temperature in our homes, and the means we have for communication with each other are all the products of human thought and effort. They buzz, beep, and hum as they do their work, and we have become so accustomed to them that we are more likely to notice the absence of their sounds than their presence. Many people are so addicted to these works of man that they become disoriented and even panicky when separated from their material goods (or gods).

Despite their dominant position in our world, the devices that we own, and that often effectively own us, are not perfect. While their designs continue to be updated to make them better and better as time passes, frequently gaining options that we never imagined could exist only a few years previous, they still malfunction, wear out, or become obsolete. If we visit a dump, we find countless items we once greeted as the hope for a brighter and more productive future, but which are now merely waste that must somehow be reprocessed or buried. Even sadder to many is when we travel through the countryside and observe buildings falling into ruin. What joy there must have been when they were built! What expectations of the builders and the buyers! Yet despite this initial enthusiasm, they have not withstood the test of time. We could discuss the tragedy of inadequate product design and of poor maintenance indefinitely, but it is time to move onward to consider the creators of the products we use.

When we see an oceangoing ship, a large building, a delicate watch, or any other sophisticated object, we recognize that the object did not come into existence through natural processes. It was both designed and manufactured through human ingenuity and effort. The vision of the inventor and the diligence of the manufacturer must both be acknowledged. Without the efforts of such people, all humanity would still be living as hunters and gatherers, with lifespans that would frequently be shortened by disease and injury. To complete our understanding of the creative process, let us consider representative professionals in three areas where the design of wares enhances our lives.

When a landscape painter, such as Susie Barstow,[1] wanted to capture a scene and to add to it the passions that she felt as she viewed the panorama, she had to lay out the whole picture in her mind. She needed to choose the correct shades of paint to produce each aspect of the painting. She had to consider how to add the depth of field that would draw the viewer into her masterpiece. Finally, she needed to craft her brush strokes to add those touches that were almost beyond the natural to show more than what was physically present to impart to the viewer the sense of awe she felt. With the design completed in her mind, she had to perform the physically demanding task of properly applying the paints in the right order and proportions to make her vision a reality on a canvas or on a wall. We can only admire the craft of such an artist.

When an architect, such as Walter Gropius[2] or Frank Lloyd Wright,[3] began to design a building, he needed to understand what the purpose of the building

---

[1] Susie Barstow was a gifted artist who painted in New York and New England during the nineteenth and twentieth centuries.
[2] Walter Gropius developed the Bauhaus school of architecture in the early twentieth century.
[3] Frank Lloyd Wright was a Wisconsin native who introduced the concept of organic architecture.

was to be. He then had to match that purpose with what seemed to him to be the appropriate structural design. That design would have to be functional and would also have to contain an element of beauty and sometimes of wonder. With his vision in mind, he next needed to confront the constraints imposed by natural factors, such as gravity, landscape, and weather, to produce a structure that would endure. Certainly, there was the visual presentation of the exterior of the building, but there was also the internal design that would cause it to be a useful structure and a joy to its owners. Detailed building drawings, often called "blueprints" because they were originally drawn or printed on blue paper, had to be developed to encompass every item that would be included in the building's construction. Whether the element of the structure was gigantic or minute, no detail could be left out, or the building might collapse or be adversely affected by the weather. Finally, to make the building a reality, materials had to be carefully selected and put into place by skilled members of the building trades. Under the watchful eye of the architect, all the work needed to be performed in the right sequence until the building matched his original vision.

Inventors, such as Thomas Edison,[4] were extremely clever people who could imagine devices that others couldn't and then turn their ideas into useful products that astounded the general public. Some men, like Sir John Fisher,[5] imagined much larger objects and brought them into existence. Fisher, for example, envisioned a battleship that was much bigger and better armored than its predecessors. Not only did he have to design the huge vessel with the help of his staff, but he also had to sell the concept to a reluctant British government. The ship he designed and built was called the "Dreadnaught" after Fisher's motto "Trust God and Dread Naught." A whole class of ships of this type was built by the British navy and other world navies in a struggle for dominance of the seas.

Moreover, we would be remiss if we considered objects without at the same time considering the persona of their creators. The mental processes that creators of objects use are a part of the creator's being, and what flows out of those processes into their art and inventions helps us to understand and some-

---

[4] Thomas Edison was an American inventor with more than a thousand patents, many of them for now-common items.
[5] Sir John "Jacky" Fisher was Admiral of the Fleet and First Sea Lord of the British Navy early in the twentieth century.

times to properly use what they have gifted to us. From the serenity and light in the works of Susie Barstow to the defiant Dreadnaught of John Fisher, we can see the relationship between the creator and the creation.

Yet, it is not only innovative ideas that are essential in a creator; he or she must also have the resources to bring those ideas to fruition. Consider the great talent we see in paintings by Leonardo da Vinci.[6] That talent also spilled over into his scientific impulses and the inventions which he drew on paper. However, in the era of Martin Luther in which da Vinci lived, the machines did not exist that could produce the precise parts necessary to transform da Vinci's elaborate drawings into operational devices. In the same way, Charles Babbage's[7] concept of a programmable digital computer could not be fully built using the technology of the nineteenth century. It is therefore essential if an object is to be produced, both a vision must be present and the ability to implement it on canvas, in steel, or in other materials must exist.

Who Could Create a Universe?

Human creators have their limitations. We are forced to recognize those limitations whenever something of human design does not meet expectations or fails. A failure could be catastrophic, as when a bridge collapses suddenly. Such a failure might result from natural forces that were not adequately considered, thereby gradually making a device or a structure unsustainable. Metal fatigue is a classic example. On the other hand, the failure could be the wasted exertion by teams of experts to create some technology that never reaches its hoped-for potential, such as harnessing the energy from fusion.[8] In all of this, we see that even as our new devices and structures become better with the passage of time, the perfection we need for the idyllic life that so many crave is never reached. In fact, often our technical advances in one field cause challenges in some other area, as when irrigation dangerously lowers the water table or when wind turbines kill birds. If human inventions made to address relatively simple matters often come up short, could there really be a creator of something as large and complex as the universe?

---

[6] Leonardo da Vinci was an Italian painter, engineer, scientist, sculptor, and architect in the late fifteenth and early sixteenth centuries.
[7] Charles Babbage was a nineteenth century English mathematician and inventor who proposed a mechanical computer.
[8] "Fusion" is the process of merging two hydrogen nuclei under conditions of extreme heat to form helium and release energy.

The Creator

The writer of the book of Hebrews had an answer to this question when he noted that "Every house is built by someone, and God is the one who built everything" (Hebrews 3:4). If God is, therefore, the ultimate creator of everything, then he must unquestionably be someone special. It is thus quite appropriate for us to learn to know who this Creator is and what his attributes (i.e., characteristics) are so that we can better understand the nature of his creation. Understanding him will help us more ably interact with his creation because, as King Solomon wrote, "The LORD has made everything for his own purpose" (Proverbs 16:4). With this introduction, we are ready to begin exploring the being of God the Creator.

Of greatest importance if we want to learn about something or someone is to have access to a reliable source of information. For most topics we might seek information from a dictionary, a history book, an online source, or a common friend. Quite reasonably, the best source of information about a person is the person himself or those who know him well. But who knows God personally or can bring him over to us so we can shake hands with him? In fact, God said to Moses, one of the few people to whom he reached out directly, "You cannot see my face, for no human may see me and live" (Exodus 33:20). Since we cannot meet God directly, we must depend on what he has revealed to us about himself. The source of that revelation is the Bible, and we will use the Bible continually as we study God and his creating activity. St. Paul assured us the Bible meets all our needs for such study when he wrote, "All Scripture is God breathed and is useful for teaching, for rebuking, for correcting, and for training in righteousness" (2 Timothy 3:16). Further discussion of the Bible as a reliable source of information can be found in the sources referenced in the Introduction.[9]

Of second importance is our recognizing that God is independent of his creation. Moses wrote, "Before the mountains were born, before you gave birth to the earth and the world, from eternity to eternity you are God" (Psalm 90:2). Surely, this is not unexpected. All human creators are separate entities from what they create. So are those animals, such as birds and beavers, that build habitats. Even the origin of machines that learn how to function better

---

[9] Brian R. Keller, *Bible*, People's Bible Teaching Series (Milwaukee: Northwestern Publishing House, 2002).

Koehler, *Christian Doctrine*, pp. 21-52.

can be traced back to human creators who were not part of the machine. While this may seem obvious, some people talk about God and the universe as if they were the same thing. This religious belief is called "pantheism" and is not compatible with what God revealed about himself in the Bible. God, therefore, is totally separate from his creation and does not depend on it in any way. This is a critical point as we look at God as a being.[10]

The Being of God

Because God is separate from his creation, we must identify and refer to him with different expressions than we use for that creation. If we describe things related to the physical world as "natural," then we need to describe that which is related to God with some other term. Since he is beyond nature in his being, we frequently use the term "supernatural"[11] when discussing him and his actions. As a result of not being a part of the physical universe, God is not "physical." In other words, a physical component, i.e., a detectable body mass, is not part of his being. Jesus said, "God is spirit, and those who worship him must worship in spirit and in truth" (John 4:24). This clarifies why we cannot know anything about God directly. None of our senses or measuring devices can detect him as they can detect the components of the physical universe. We cannot poke and probe him to gauge his size, his abilities, or his limitations as we can with physical objects. St. Paul described God as "the blessed and only ruler, the King of kings and Lord of lords, who alone has immortality, who lives in unapproachable light, whom no one has seen or is able to see. To him be honor and power forever! Amen" (1 Timothy 6:15,16).

Even more frustrating to our notion of our own astuteness is that we cannot grasp anything about God directly with our minds. There is nothing "self-evident" about him. Concerning this, St. Paul wrote, "Oh, the depth of the riches and wisdom and knowledge of God! How unsearchable are his judgments and how untraceable his ways! 'For who has known the mind of the Lord, or who has been his adviser?'" (Romans 11:33,34). God was even more emphatic about himself when he said, "Certainly my plans are not your plans, and your ways are not my ways, declares the LORD. Just as the heavens are higher than the earth, so my ways are higher than your ways, and my plans are higher than

---

[10] Arthur A. Eggert, *Simply Lutheran* (Milwaukee: Northwestern Publishing House, 2020), pp. 43-56.

[11] "Supernatural," as used in this book, means "not governed by the laws of nature." It does not mean "magic" or "fantasy."

your plans" (Isaiah 55:8,9). The Creator of the universe has made it clear that he does not need second guessing by one of his creatures, namely man. We have no standing to question his competence. The LORD said, "Woe to anyone who argues against the potter who formed him. He is just a potsherd among the broken pieces of pottery on the ground. Does clay say to its potter, 'What are you making? Your work looks like something made by a potter with no hands'?" (Isaiah 45:9). *We must deal with God the Creator on his terms, not ours.*

Finally, we should give heed to God's description of himself contained in the name he used to identify himself to Moses. Although he does indeed often refer to himself by various names, including "God," "LORD," the "Lord God Almighty," the "LORD of Armies," "the God of Israel," and the "King of kings and Lord of lords," yet one name stands out from all others, the name "I AM."[12] God exists in and of himself, and it is by his existence that he most desires to be identified. There is none other like him. A psalmist wrote, "High above all the nations is the LORD. His glory towers above the heavens. Who is like the LORD our God? He is seated on high" (Psalm 113:4,5). This naturally leads us to consider the qualifications of one with such a name to be the Creator of all.

The Knowledge of God

As we have already seen, a creator of any object needs both the knowledge to design what he desires to create and the resources, including the ability, to implement that design. Let us consider the area of design first. The basis of all design is a knowledge of what must be present in the final product so it will meet the need for which it is being designed. A building, for example, must have enough space for the activities that will occur within it. A toothbrush must be sturdy enough to clean the teeth without damaging the gums. Kitchen cabinets must not be so high or so deep that their users cannot reach what has been stored in them. Computer programs must not have excessive "bells and whistles" while lacking critical features. The designer therefore

---

[12] But Moses said to God, "If I go to the Israelites and say to them, 'The God of your fathers has sent me to you,' and they ask me, 'What is his name?' what should I say to them?" So God replied to Moses, "I AM WHO I AM." He also said, "You will say this to the Israelites: I AM has sent me to you." (Exodus 3:13,14)

must be a methodical analyst as well as having a vision for how the components of the product will work harmoniously together. Many products, from footwear to battlecruisers, are under-designed because their creators lack sufficient knowledge about their intended use and their operational constraints.

When we examine his attributes, we indeed find that the LORD, the God of the Bible, has the necessary knowledge to carry out the monumental task of creating the universe. A psalmist wrote, "Great is our Lord and mighty in power. To his understanding there is no limit" (Psalm 147:5). The writer to the Hebrews declared, "There is no creature hidden from him, but everything is uncovered and exposed to the eyes of him to whom we will give an account" (Hebrews 4:13). King Solomon wrote, "The eyes of the LORD are everywhere, watching evil people as well as the good" (Proverbs 15:3).[13] Jesus pointed out that God is aware of even the smallest things when he said, "Are not two sparrows sold for a small coin? Yet not one of them will fall to the ground without the knowledge and consent of your Father. And even the hairs of your head are all numbered" (Matthew 10:29,30). Hairs and sparrows have little value, yet the Bible declares that even such apparently insignificant things are not ignored by God. On the other hand, the Bible also tells us that God has control of the things of galactic proportions. "'To whom can you compare me as if we were equals?' says the Holy One. Lift up your eyes to the heavens, and see who created these things. See who brings out their army in great number and calls them all by name. Because of his great strength and mighty power, not one of them is missing" (Isaiah 40:25,26). When he spoke to Job (Job 38-41) because the latter became rebellious due to his suffering, the LORD revealed a thorough knowledge of the forces of nature.

In the inerrant revelation about himself that he has given us in the Scriptures through the chosen writers whom he verbally inspired, the LORD was not shy about placing before us his credentials as a being having complete knowledge. Regarding things both huge and tiny, he has attested to the overwhelming knowledge that he had to employ in creating the universe. If his understanding has no limit, then he cannot be caught by surprise. There could have been no danger in his forgetting some detail that would have made the universe less than satisfactory. King David endorsed this statement when he declared that God knows things even before they happen. He wrote, "Before

---

[13] Certainly, the writer to the Hebrews and Solomon were not claiming that God has physical eyes to see everywhere, but they were using figures of speech as when we say, "The angels really must have been watching over me today."

there is a word on my tongue, you, LORD, already know it completely" (Psalm 139:4). We call this incredible attribute of God his "omniscience."

The Power of God

Since the beginning of the nineteenth century, the power and capabilities of human inventions have grown rapidly. Primitive machines (such as water wheels) in the era of the American Revolution have been replaced by complex machines that require whole buildings to house (such as nuclear reactors). Transportation devices that could barely move themselves (such as the first railroad locomotives) have become the forerunners of planes, ships, and trains that can move more consumer goods than any one person could use in a lifetime. Man has even created nuclear weapons that can destroy whole cities. Indeed, the inventions created by humankind are impressive. Nevertheless, human inventions are all prone to failure in one manner or another due to less-than-perfect design and workmanship. Moreover, they are still small in power when compared to the sun, a hurricane, or an earthquake. It is therefore natural for people to gauge power by the capability of human inventions on one hand and, on the other hand, by those things that are so far beyond human ability to address they seem uncontrollable by any means. Many people tend to place God's ability to affect the physical realm somewhere between that of human devices and that of massive natural phenomena. From this positioning, they conclude God did not have sufficient power to create everything that exists, but rather he is limited to managing things as best he can. Based on the physical and political condition of the world, some even doubt he is very effective at what he can do.

In stark contrast to this shallow view of God, the Lord God Almighty, whom the Bible proclaims as the Creator of the universe, is not limited by human speculation. He is truly a being who can do anything he pleases. Moses said, "The LORD your God is God of Gods and Lord of Lords, the great God, the mighty one and the awesome one, who does not show favoritism and does not take a bribe" (Deuteronomy 10:17). A psalmist wrote, "Yes, I know that the LORD is great. Our Lord is greater than all gods. The LORD does whatever he pleases in the heavens and on the earth, in the seas and in all the depths" (Psalm 135:5,6). Another psalmist wrote, "Let all the earth fear the LORD. Let all the inhabitants of the world revere him. For he said, 'Let it be,' and it was!

He gave a command, and there it stood" (Psalm 33:8,9). Other biblical speakers and writers echoed the picture of God's overwhelming power. Isaiah wrote, "For the LORD of Armies has made plans, and who can stop him? His hand is stretched out, and who can turn it back?" (Isaiah 14:27). The angel Gabriel said, "For nothing will be impossible for God" (Luke 1:37). Jesus said, "For people, it is impossible, but not for God, because all things are possible for God" (Mark 10:27). Later he said, "*Abba*, Father, everything is possible for you" (Mark 14:36). St. Paul wrote, "How surpassingly great his power is for us who believe. It is as great as the working of his mighty strength" (Ephesians 1:19,20). From Moses to St. Paul, God proclaimed that his power is great enough to accomplish anything he wills to do, as we will look at more closely in chapters 3 through 5. He willed to create the universe, and there can be no question that he had the power to do so.

We have seen from his revelation that the LORD has both the knowledge and power to do as he pleases, including to create the universe. There is no one like him. If we think about the biblical description of just these few attributes of God, we are forced to reevaluate our view of the being of God. He presents such an overpowering image that our minds want to reduce him to something they can hold and manipulate. We simply cannot do that. God blows the top off our curve of understanding. We need to accept his incredible knowledge and power by faith, not try to bound them by things with which we are familiar. As he says about himself, "I AM." He is, and we are left to be amazed at the being of God.

But now we must move on. We must consider why he became involved in the universe-creating business. The universe is a big place, even for an all-powerful God (at least from our point of view). In the next chapter we will look at God in the period when he had not yet created the world, and we will explore what the Bible reveals about him in the realm of eternity.

2

From Eternity

We saw in the last chapter that the LORD is a God who knows everything and has unlimited power. Being human, of course, we are curious and want to know more. It is natural for us to ask where this God existed and what he was doing before he created the universe. While these questions may seem reasonable from a human point of view, they are not easy to answer because God is not like us. All our reference points for understanding events are in the physical world that God created, but he is not of that created world. Moreover, God chose not to reveal much information to us about his activities apart from his interaction with his creation. Given these limitations, we will next consider what God has revealed in the Bible because it is essential background to his creating activities.

Eternity

We begin with the word "eternity." What is it? People make statements such as, "It took an eternity for the baggage to appear after we landed." In this idiom, "eternity" may only have been a brief time interval in terms of the human lifespan or of the age of the Earth, but it seemed very long because it was preventing the speaker from doing something else that would have been more enjoyable or more useful. This usage of the word "eternity," however, is not what the Bible means when it employs the word to describe something about God. *Eternity is not really a length of time but a condition of existence that is outside of our concept of time.* The Levitical chorus sang, "Stand up! Bless the LORD your God, who is from eternity to eternity" (Nehemiah 9:5). They meant God is from before time as we know it to after time as we know it.

It is at this point that our understanding begins to be challenged because we need to know more about the nature of time, even though we normally take time as a given. God is what might be called "immutable" or "invariant." Stated another way, God does not change with time. A psalmist wrote, "Long ago you laid a foundation for the earth, and the heavens are the work of your hands. They will perish, but you remain. All of them wear out like a garment. Like clothing you will change them, and they will be changed. But you are the same, and your years will never end" (Psalm 102:25-27). This reveals one of the problems we face in trying to understand God. We define time in terms of change. If something does not change, then effectively time has not passed for it. People in photos do not age. They always appear the same as they did on the day when the photo was taken.[1] We might say they are "frozen in time." Because God does not change with the passage of time as we comprehend it, we struggle to understand how he can be the dynamic being the Scriptures reveal him to be and still not change. Nevertheless, the LORD emphatically stated, "Certainly I, the LORD, do not change. That is why you, sons of Jacob, have not come to an end." (Malachi 3:6).

Because our common definition of time does not fit with the being of God as he is revealed in the Scriptures, we must reconsider how we understand eternity. We must view God as dwelling in eternity as we dwell in space and time. In fact, scientists have learned that physical space and time are interrelated, and thus they might better be collectively called "spacetime."[2] In the same way that we call our realm of existence "spacetime," we call God's realm of existence "eternity." A major distinction between the two is that our realm was created by God and has the properties that he assigned to it. His realm is an inherent part of his existence, and it was not created.[3] As we have previously noted, Moses wrote, "Before the mountains were born, before you gave birth to the earth and the world, from eternity to eternity you are God" (Psalm 90:2). The phrase "eternity to eternity" is used to indicate God's existence from when there were no created things until when the current universe will no longer exist. The LORD will always be the same and will always dwell

---

[1] In 1890 Oscar Wilde published a novel entitled *The Picture of Dorian Gray*, which dealt with the dichotomy of a person being frozen in time and yet living. In his novel the subject *in* the picture aged but the subject *of* the picture did not.

[2] Sean Carroll, *Mysteries of Modern Physics: Time*, The Great Courses (Chantilly, Virginia: The Teaching Company, 2013), Lecture 2.

[3] This statement is extremely important. If the existence of the realm in which God dwells were independent of him, then he would be limited by something that was not himself and therefore would not be almighty.

in this "eternity." King David likewise used this phrase to recognize the utter changelessness of God, "Blessed are you, LORD, the God of Israel, our father, from eternity to eternity. To you, O LORD, belong greatness, power, glory, victory, and majesty, because everything in the heavens and on the earth belongs to you. You, LORD, are exalted as head above everything" (1 Chronicles 29:10,11).

Since eternity is not something that exists within our spacetime, we have no way to examine it apart from the revelation given in the Bible. When St. Paul said of God "who alone has immortality, who lives in unapproachable light, whom no one has seen or is able to see" (1 Timothy 6:16), he was emphasizing the inaccessibility of eternity from our realm of existence, i.e., our spacetime. In the Bible sometimes the created "highest heaven" is used to help people understand God's separation from man in a realm of his own.[4] King Solomon declared in his prayer, "In truth, the heavens, even the highest heaven, cannot contain you" (1 Kings 8:27). Jesus also emphasized how God is separated from our domain when he said, "No one has ascended into heaven, except the one who descended from heaven, the Son of Man, who is in heaven" (John 3:13). It is only through the revelation given by the Holy Spirit in the Scriptures that we have any knowledge about the domain of eternity.

The Bible additionally uses the Hebrew word *olam*, often translated as "everlasting," to describe some actions of God. The word does not necessarily mean forever, i.e., unbounded time. For example, the LORD said to Abraham, "My covenant will be marked on your flesh as an everlasting covenant" (Genesis 17:13). The covenant of circumcision was not a covenant that would last beyond the end of the world, but only until the time when Jesus came and created a new covenant in his blood that would endure until the end of the world. At other times, the Bible does use "everlasting" as comparable to "eternity," such as when "eternity" is being used to refer to something continuing beyond the end of the world. For example, the LORD said, "Israel will be saved

---

[4] Ancient people thought there were three levels of heaven. The lowest level was where the birds flew and where the clouds floated. The "second heaven" was where the sun, moon, and the stars traveled. The "third heaven" was where God and his holy ones lived. The penmen of the Bible used people's imperfect understanding to try to generally convey what could not be precisely explained, namely the dwelling place of God. "Heavens" is often used as a plural in the Bible to indicate God's power over all regions above the earth.

by the LORD with everlasting salvation. You will not be ashamed or disgraced for all eternity" (Isaiah 45:17). The songs of ascent (Psalms 120-134)[5] often use "eternity" in this sense, namely, as beyond the end of time, not as the dwelling place of God, e.g., "from now to eternity" (Psalm 121:8).

God's "Personal" Acts

Even though we are forced to concede we do not understand the eternal realm in which God exists, we might still wonder what God was doing when he had no physical universe with which to interact. We tend to equate having nothing to do with being bored. Since it is hard for us to imagine an omniscient and omnipotent God twiddling his spiritual thumbs in boredom, we might feel that he must have been doing something, and we would like to know what that something was. In fact, the Bible reveals God did act in eternity,[6] but it only gives us very limited information about his actions. From this information, however, we can divide his actions into two types.

The first type of action is that which occurs among the persons of the Trinity and which does not extend beyond the Trinity.[7] We call these God's "personal internal acts."[8] The first of these acts about which we have received revelation is that of the person of the Father having begotten the person of the Son. This act of begetting happened in the realm of eternity, and we do not understand it. Nevertheless, it is well documented in the Bible. Jesus said, "For God so loved the world that he gave his only-begotten Son, that whoever believes in him shall not perish, but have eternal life" (John 3:16) and "The one who does not believe is condemned already, because he has not believed in the name of the only-begotten Son of God" (John 3:18). St. John wrote, "This is how God's love for us was revealed: God has sent his only-begotten Son into the world so that we may live through him" (1 John 4:9). Certainly, we would like to understand more clearly what "begotten" means because the

---

[5] The Psalms of Ascent were traditionally sung by the people of Israel as groups traveled up the road to Jerusalem or climbed up the temple mount for festival celebrations.

[6] Selecting the appropriate verb tense to use to describe God's actions in eternity is challenging because for God the present is always the appropriate tense, but for our limited understanding of eternity sometimes the past tense needs to be employed.

[7] Richard D. Balge, *Trinity*, People's Bible Teachings series (Milwaukee: Northwestern Publishing House, 2001).

Koehler, *Christian Doctrine*, pp. 64-68.

[8] A. L. Graebner, *Outlines of Doctrinal Theology* (St. Louis: Concordia Publishing House, 1910).

preincarnate Son, the second person of the Trinity, had no mother.[9] We will need to wait until Jesus returns to ask him.

The second personal internal act of God is the persons of the Father and of the Son "spirating" (breathing out) the person of the Holy Spirit. This act is also called "procession." Again, we do not understand how it occurred in eternity, but we have solid biblical statements that both the Father and the Son are bound to the Holy Spirit in this manner. Jesus said, "The Counselor, the Holy Spirit, whom the Father will send in my name, will teach you all things and remind you of everything I told you" (John 14:26) and "When the Counselor comes, whom I will send to you from the Father—the Spirit of truth, who proceeds from the Father—he will testify about me" (John 15:26). St. Paul wrote, "But you are not in the sinful flesh but in the spirit, if indeed God's Spirit lives in you. And if someone does not have the Spirit of Christ, that person does not belong to Christ" (Romans 8:9) and "Because you are sons, God sent the Spirit of his Son into our hearts to shout, "*Abba*, Father!'" (Galatians 4:6). No other personal internal acts of the Trinity are revealed to us in the Bible. We must be very careful to believe only what is revealed and not speculate about the interpersonal acts of God, lest we morph our perception of God into another form and make an idol of him as did the Israelites (Exodus 32:1-6).

God's "Preparatory" Acts

It is hard to imagine God needing to prepare for anything. Because he never changes and knows everything, how can he not always be ready for any situation? Nevertheless, there are three acts that God performed before creation ("before" from our perspective) as stage-setting acts for his creation of the universe. These have come to be called "essential internal acts."[10] They are internal to God because they occurred in eternity, but they led to actions that would be seen in the created world.

---

[9] Not understanding the nature of the term "begotten" as used in the Bible can lead to major doctrinal error. Mohammed misunderstood this Christian teaching because he was illiterate. He believed that the Trinity consisted of the Father, Jesus, and Miriam (alias the Virgin Mary), who had been the sister of Moses.

[10] Essential internal acts of God are sometimes called "decrees." These "decrees" made in eternity became effective in time at the point when they were necessary to carry out God's purpose.

The first of these acts is called the "decree of creation." St. Paul referred to it in addressing the Athenians, "From one man, he made every nation of mankind to live over the entire face of the earth. He determined the appointed times and the boundaries where they would live" (Acts 17:26). The LORD had planned out such things as the characteristics of each nation before any nation existed. A psalmist directs thanks "To him who by his understanding made the heavens" (Psalm 136:5). This assures us God did not create the universe haphazardly. He understood what he was doing when he began. Another psalmist wrote, "How many are your works, O LORD! In wisdom you made them all" (Psalm 104:24). Not only did the LORD understand what he was doing, but he did it based on the wise counsel existing within the Trinity from eternity. Moses recorded that before God created man, he said, "Let us make man in our image, according to our likeness" (Genesis 1:26). Because God does not change, this was not some spur-of-the-moment decision for the purpose of answering the question, "What should we do now?" No, it was part of God's creation "blueprint" from eternity.

Moreover, because God is omniscient, he knew his creature man would rebel against him and would fall into sin. Therefore, he performed a second essential internal act, namely, the "decree of redemption."[11] God prepared a response to man's future actions. God is perfect,[12] and he cannot tolerate imperfection within his creation. A psalmist wrote, "Yes, the LORD approves of the way of the righteous, but the way of the wicked will perish" (Psalm 1:6). His perfection meant God had to be prepared to deal with man's rebellion. Anything less than perfection did not meet his standard and therefore fell under his wrath. His action to resolve the impending rebellion of man would lead to something totally mind-boggling from a human vantage point, because the very nature of God meant that he had to punish sin. The LORD said to Ezekiel, "The soul who sins is the one who will die" (Ezekiel 18:4). King David wrote, "For you are not a God who takes pleasure in evil. With you the wicked cannot dwell. The arrogant cannot stand before your eyes. You hate all evildoers. You put to death those who speak lies" (Psalm 5:4-6).[13]

---

[11] The "Decree of Redemption" was God's entire plan of salvation for mankind.
[12] [Jesus said,] "So then, be perfect, as your heavenly Father is perfect." (Matthew 5:48)
[13] The terms "perfect," "holy," and "righteous" are often used interchangeably, but each of them has a narrower meaning that is sometimes important. "Holy" means to be totally dedicated to something. The high priest of Israel wore a banner on his turban that read "Holy to the LORD." (Exodus 28:36) "Perfect" means to conform exactly to a standard, such as a "perfect sphere." "Righteous" means to be both civilly and morally perfect, i.e., above reproach. One is not righteous if one acts perfect legally, but for sinful reasons, like the Phari-

God's plan to deal with mankind's rebellion, a plan already existent in eternity, would be unprecedented and would again involve creative acts by the LORD. In chapter 8, we will consider this plan in terms of its overall effect but particularly in terms of God's creating acts that were involved in it.

God's third essential internal act is his predestination of those who would be given eternal life, that is, the "decree of predestination." This was an act by God that has caused much mental anguish in the Christian church over many centuries because God's predestination decree seems at odds with his second essential internal act, namely, his intent to save all mankind. We will briefly consider predestination in this chapter to the degree that it is involved with creation, but other sources should be consulted for a deeper understanding of the doctrine[14] and of the controversy in the Lutheran church concerning it.[15]

The doctrine of predestination was outlined by St. Paul when he wrote, "Blessed be the God and Father of our Lord Jesus Christ, who has blessed us in Christ with every spiritual blessing in the heavenly places. He did this when he chose us in Christ before the foundation of the world, so that we would be holy and blameless in his sight. In love he predestined us to be adopted as his sons through Jesus Christ. He did this in accordance with the good purpose of his will, and for the praise of his glorious grace, which he has graciously given us in the one he loves" (Ephesians 1:3-6). St. Paul went into more detail when he wrote to the Romans, "We know that all things work together for the good of those who love God, for those who are called according to his purpose, because those God foreknew, he also predestined to be conformed to the image of his Son, so that he would be the firstborn among many brothers. And those he predestined, he also called. Those he called, he also justified. And those he justified, he also glorified" (Romans 8:28-30). St. Paul continued, "For I am convinced that neither death nor life, neither angels nor rulers, neither things present nor things to come, nor powerful forces, neither height nor depth, nor

---

sees did. When reading passages in the Scriptures, one must examine carefully how the writer is using these terms.

[14] John A. Molstad, *Predestination*, People's Bible Teachings series (Milwaukee: Northwestern Publishing House, 1997).

Koehler, *Christian Doctrine*, pp. 240-246.

[15] John M. Brenner, "The Election Controversy Among Lutherans in the Twentieth Century" (http://epublications.marquette.edu/dissertations_mu/204).

anything else in creation, will be able to separate us from the love of God in Christ Jesus our Lord" (Romans 8:38,39).

These passages written by St. Paul present the key ideas in the doctrine of predestination. The predestination (also called "election") of those who would become Christ's adherents and thus be saved occurred in eternity. The choosing was done "in Christ," i.e., through the saving work of Christ. Not only did God elect some to be saved, but he set in place all the steps necessary to make that salvation an accomplished fact for the elect. Finally, he planned to protect his elect so that nothing in the physical or spiritual realms could steal them away from him. For this reason, St. Paul could say that all things work together for good for the elect. Yet there is one more verse from St. Paul's writings that must be considered, "Even when you were dead in your trespasses and the uncircumcision of your flesh, God made you alive with Christ by forgiving us all our trespasses" (Colossians 2:13). God did not elect people for salvation due to their sterling character, for even the elect were spiritually dead, but he elected them solely through Christ.

The whole process outlined by St. Paul could only happen due to God's creating activity. When the LORD elected someone for salvation, he planned everything that needed to be done for that salvation to occur. Through his creative work he placed everything correctly in space and time to ensure that the countless steps required to position a person to be brought to faith and to keep that person in faith would transpire. Perhaps God lined everything up like a complex billiard shot on the first day of creation. Perhaps he has tweaked nature as time passes. Perhaps he has done a little of both.[16] We do not know, and we should not care. All of it was already set in eternity.

And now the stage is set. We have examined the Creator and found that he has always existed and that he is all-knowing and all-powerful. We have considered his dwelling in the realm of eternity. We have briefly looked at what the Bible reveals about the personal internal acts of God. We have looked at his preparatory acts as he readied himself to call the universe into existence. In the next chapter the curtain goes up on the greatest production that has ever been or ever will be staged.

---

[16] This is certainly only a description of how God would need to act from a human viewpoint. From God's vantage point in eternity, however, things might appear altogether different.

3

In the Beginning

The place was nowhere. The time was no time. We are told that it was the beginning. "In the beginning, God created the heavens and the earth" (Genesis 1:1). What was going on here? What does it mean? The explanation is utterly amazing![1]

The Incredible Start

God was dwelling in eternity. There was nothing else. We might wonder whether at some point God's preset alarm went off, and he arose to go out to an empty patch of nearby space to begin his creation of the world. How else could we explain his choice of a particular instant to begin creating? Nevertheless, it didn't happen that way. Instead, he implemented the decree of creation discussed in chapter 2. There was no empty space. Space itself has a structure even if it is apparently empty.[2] This discovery forces us to consider a disturbing possibility. If empty space existed before God began creating, then he would not be the creator of everything because he would not have created space. He would simply have been a being who was using something that already existed. Consequently, God would not have been the only thing that had no beginning; space also would have existed. And if God were not the only thing that was preexistent before his acts of creating, what would that mean for our confidence that there are no other supernatural objects or beings that have permanent independent existence? Our minds would wonder whether there were things relevant to us that God was not telling us about the "be-

---

[1] Arthur A. Eggert, "Genesis 1 and Science," *Wisconsin Lutheran Quarterly*, Vol. 117, No. 4 (Fall 2020), pp. 243-268.
[2] Carroll, *Time*, Lectures 22-23.

fore creation" universe, if we might hesitantly use that concept. This would not be good, and fortunately this was not the case.

In the beginning when God "created," there was no space in existence. He needed to make space where there had previously been only non-existence so he would have a place to insert his creation. Because of this, he would be responsible for the existence of space in the same way he was responsible for the existence of everything that he put into that space. Moreover, there was no time before God created it. Unless revealed, the happenings in eternity are unknowable, but they did not involve the concept of time with which we are familiar. If they had, then God would be dependent on time in determining when he could act. He would not be independent, but he would be like us, his creatures, who are constrained by a timeline where events move relentlessly in one direction. Preexistent space or preexistent time would to some degree constrain the actions of God and make him somewhat less than almighty. Because of this, God had to create both space and time, i.e., the spacetime envelope in which all creation exists as was introduced in chapter 2, so he could truly be the "Creator God" introduced in chapter 1.

If we are to comprehend what happened at creation, we must rely on the original Hebrew text of the Bible.[3] The word for "create" in Genesis 1:1 is *bara'*, which in this context where it is constrained by "in the beginning" and is an action of God, must mean to create out of nothing (i.e., *ex nihilo*).[4] This is the correct translation that is consistent with its meaning when the word appears elsewhere in the Hebrew text. What happened at creation certainly taxes our understanding. We cannot imagine the non-existence of space. Space is the three orthogonal directions we have learned to understand and love—right and left, back and forth, up and down. Since there was no space before the creation, what was there? This is our question, but it is a nonsensical question because it is in our frame of reference that did not exist at creation. In the same way, there was no passage of time "before" God's creation. God's creation not only brought into existence the matter of the universe, but also the space that held it and the ability for it to change via time.

Faced with something that is not compatible with our view of the universe, we are tempted to turn to science to give us rational answers. The methods of

---

[3] Arthur A. Eggert, "Creation vs. Science – The Underlying Principles", presented to the Southeast Pastor-Teacher Conference of the Michigan District, Westland, Michigan, February 2011.

[4] Samuel H. Nafzger *et al.*, eds., *Confessing the Gospel*, Vol. 1 (St. Louis: Concordia Publishing House, 2017), pp. 125-129.

science will be discussed in chapter 11, but the results of those methods as they apply to the issues raised by creation will be used as we proceed. Scientists have indeed thrown enormous amounts of instrumentation, computing power, and cleverness at the problem of the origin of the universe. They had considered and rejected many ideas before someone proposed that, based on all the evidence, the universe must have exploded into existence from a very small, highly compressed sphere of energy, little bigger than a pinpoint, and rapidly expanded to become what we now observe.[5] Such an idea seems outrageously stupid. Opposition to it was initially strong in the scientific community, and its detractors called it the "big bang theory" in derision. The name stuck, and more and more evidence was found that was consistent with it. By the end of the twentieth century, it was a well-established cosmic model for which an incredibly detailed timeline had been developed. In curiosity, we might ask, "What is the central claim of this model?" Scientists postulate that "before" the big bang occurred, there was no space or time as we know it. The explosion generated the spacetime envelope in which the universe exists. How interesting! This is exactly the concept we are struggling with regarding God's creating activities. While the big bang theory does not support divine creation, it does show that even diligent scientific investigators have concluded that space and time are not invariant entities that have always existed in the form we know them. This is the same conclusion we are forced to draw from the study of the Bible. Space and time had a beginning, and the Bible tells us that that beginning was a creative act of God.

The Initial State of the Earth

The Bible next gives us a short description of what the creation would have appeared like to a human observer. "The earth was undeveloped and empty. Darkness covered the surface of the deep" (Genesis 1:2a). In one way, this is what we would expect of a construction project. The contractor orders the supplies, and they are delivered and piled about in an apparently haphazard manner, awaiting the start of the building process. On the other hand, we might have expected God's decree of creation would have caused everything to pop into existence instantly in totally perfect final form. However, we must

---

[5] David Christian, *Big History: The Big Bang, Life on Earth, and the Rise of Humanity*, The Great Courses (Chantilly, Virginia: The Teaching Company, 2008), Lectures 5-6.

remember the decree of creation was an internal act of God that he had to implement through bringing the physical universe into existence. God in his wisdom did not decree a pop-up creation, and he did not think it necessary to explain to us why he didn't.

God, however, did record in the Bible some additional information about what he was doing during the beginning of the creating process. "And the Spirit of God was hovering over the surface of the waters" (Genesis 1:2b). In this verse, we see the result of one of God's personal internal acts. The use of "God" in both the Old and New Testaments often refers to God the Father, and the Israelites thought of God as their Father. Malachi wrote, "Don't we all have one Father? Hasn't one God created us?" (Malachi 2:10). In the Nicene Creed and the Apostles' Creed we speak of "God the Father" as the "maker of heaven and earth." In Genesis 1:2, the third person of the Trinity, the Holy Spirit, is specifically mentioned. We saw in chapter 2 that he eternally proceeds from God the Father and God the Son. By this point in the creation process, already two of the three persons of the Trinity have been mentioned. Although God as a being is a spirit, the mention of the "Spirit of God" cannot be understood as a synonym for "God" in verse 1 because it differs from all the references to God associated with all the creative acts that follow in Genesis 1. We see the distinction between the Father and the Holy Spirit clearly in passages such as, "The LORD spoke to Moses: 'Look, here is Bezalel, the son of Uri, the son of Hur, from the tribe of Judah. I have called him by name. I have filled him with the Spirit of God, with wisdom, understanding, and knowledge, and with skill in all kinds of crafts'" (Exodus 31:1-3).

We also learn from this second verse of Genesis that the creation was initially enmeshed in a watery chaos, which is the real meaning of the Hebrew word translated here as "water." At this point in God's creative process, we should avoid drawing any conclusions about the form and the organization of the materials that were present. They existed, and the Holy Spirit was interfacing with them.

In the next line of the sacred text, God reveals several critical details, "And God said, 'Let there be light: and there was light'" (Genesis 1:3). The first thing that we learn is that God "spoke." He interacted with his creation by means of words. God, of course, is a spirit and has no physical mouth. The inanimate material to which he "spoke" had no ears. Prior to this, all God's communication was within the Godhead, but now with the creation in progress, he was addressing some other entity. We have no information about

God's internal communication, but here we learn that God's external communication with created things is like one person speaking to another. We might ask, "Did God utter words having sound, or was the speaking done in a different manner?" Inanimate matter cannot understand human speech, at least as far as we know, so how did it understand God? Indeed, was he speaking to what he had already created or did the light come into existence from nothing at his word? These are all good questions, but God did not reveal enough for us to answer them. Yet, we should not be dismayed; what happened is clear. God addressed the inanimate, and it responded by doing his will.

To complete the picture of the beginning of creation, let us review what we can know from other portions of Scripture, namely, that the second person of the Trinity was also involved in the creative process. St. John wrote, "In the beginning was the Word, and the Word was with God, and the Word was God. He was with God in the beginning. Through him everything was made, and without him not one thing was made that has been made" (John 1:1-3). St. John here used "Word" to indicate God the Son. We learn upon further study that the "Word" in this sense means "revelation" and that the early Christian church often referred to the Son as the "word of God's revelation." Jesus said, "No one knows who the Son is except the Father, and no one knows who the Father is except the Son and anyone to whom the Son wants to reveal him" (Luke 10:22). God the Father begets God the Son in eternity, and God the Son acts as the creating agent of the Father at creation and as the revealer of God to mankind. This is the reason the internal acts of God in eternity are important.

The Significance of Light

God's first act in bringing order to the chaotic new world was his calling forth of light. His selection of this act is an extremely important message in itself. We know little about the realm of eternity because we cannot see into it. One might say that it is "dark" to us. Upon completion of the temple, King Solomon acknowledged this situation when he said, "The LORD has said that he dwells in thick darkness. I have truly built a majestic house for you, a place for you to dwell forever" (1 Kings 8:12,13). However, God himself is light, not darkness. St. John wrote about what he had heard from Jesus, "This is the message we heard from him and proclaim to you: God is light. In him there is no darkness at all. If we say we have fellowship with him but still walk in darkness, we are lying and do not put the truth into practice. But if we walk in the light, just as he is in the light, we have fellowship with one another, and the blood of Jesus Christ, his Son, cleanses us from all sin" (1 John 1:5-7). The bringing forth of light at the beginning of time (i.e., "time" from the human perspective) showed that the God of light would not hide himself from his creation but that he would be "visible" because we can see in the light but not in the darkness. More will be said about God's visibility as we proceed.

The physical light on the first day of the creation, moreover, foreshadowed the great spiritual light that comes from God. God's psalmists spoke of that light. King David wrote, "Yes, you light my lamp, O LORD. My God turns my darkness to light" (Psalm 18:28) and "The precepts of the LORD are right. They give joy to the heart. The commandment of the LORD is bright. It gives light to the eyes" (Psalm 19:8). Certainly, David was not speaking of physical light here, but he was using the properties of such light to declare how God enlightens the soul. The great acrostic psalm says, "Your words are a lamp for my feet and a light for my path" (Psalm 119:105).

The light given by God in the Old Testament was not all the illumination he would provide; a greater light was to come. Isaiah wrote, "The people walking in darkness have seen a great light. For those living in the land of the shadow of death, the light has dawned" (Isaiah 9:2). Death is here pictured as a shadow that hung over all mankind. A shadow is dark, and this darkness needed to be removed by an act of God. Jesus, God the Son in human form, made that very clear. Indeed, as God, he was bringing a spiritual light into the world, a light the world had not previously known, just as God the Father had brought physical light into the world that it had not known. Jesus said, "I am the Light of the World. Whoever follows me will never walk in darkness, but will have the light of life" (John 8:12). Certainly, Jesus wanted to enlighten the world. He was the source of the light, but those who trusted in him needed to reflect that light, just as the moon reflects the light of the sun. Jesus said to his followers, "In the same way let your light shine in people's presence, so that they may see your good works and glorify your Father who is in heaven" (Matthew 5:16). Our being children of God's light is that important.

At the command of the LORD, light appeared. It obeyed God's word and came into existence. We might ask how this could be, since there was no usual natural source for the light—no sun, no star, no candle. Yet the light was there.

In the Beginning

But what is light? Our best model of light is that it is electromagnetic radiation, i.e., oscillating electric and magnetic fields that move in a particular direction.[6] The oscillations (i.e., "waves") can be as short as one-thousandth of a nanometer (called "gamma rays") and as long as 100,000 kilometers (called "extremely low frequency" waves). The visible portion of the electromagnetic spectrum is only a tiny slice from 400 to 800 nanometers because it is the only portion of the spectrum to which the human eye is sensitive. What portion of the spectrum God created on the first day is unknown because he did not reveal this information to us.

Some might say that without a localized physical source, there can be no light. Scientists, however, have shown that this is not true. If we turned a microwave receiver in any direction, we would pick up background radiation.[7] This background "light" is called the "cosmic microwave background," and it is always traveling in all directions throughout space. Although scientists link the generation of this radiation to a specific occurrence in the aftermath of the big bang, nevertheless, it is radiation without a localized physical source. Consequently, the ability of unsourced radiation, i.e., light, to exist in the physical universe must be accepted because it has been observed. The almighty God was certainly able to create unsourced radiation just as he created everything else that we observe in the world. In this case, careful scientific observations led to a discovery that eliminated a challenge previously made to the biblical account of a divine action during creation. This example demonstrates why we should not concern ourselves with such scientific challenges, because scientific thinking changes as new evidence is discovered.

When God reviewed his initial creative work, he determined that it met his standards of quality. "God saw that the light was good" (Genesis 1:4a). How could we be surprised at this? All God's work is good! King David wrote, "The heavens tell about the glory of God. The expanse of the sky proclaims the work of his hands" (Psalm 19:1). Another psalmist wrote, "Yes, the word of the LORD is right, and everything he does is trustworthy" (Psalm 33:4).

God next designated an area where the light was allowed and an area where there was only darkness. "He separated the light from the darkness" (Genesis

---

[6] Peter Paul Urone and Roger Hinrichs, *College Physics* (Houston: OpenStax, 2019), pp. 951-969.
[7] Felix J. Lockman, *Radio Astronomy: Observing the Invisible Universe*, The Great Courses (Chantilly, Virginia: The Teaching Company, 2008), Lecture 13.

1:4b). We do not know how he accomplished this task or what it meant, but it did set the stage for what he was about to do. "God called the light 'day,' and the darkness he called 'night'" (Genesis 1:5a).[8] This action established a period for work and a period for rest. Jesus referred to this concept allegorically when he said, "I must do the works of him who sent me while it is day. Night is coming when no one can work" (John 9:4). This act also allowed God to close his first period of creation.

The "Days" of Creation

God conveyed that he created the time component of spacetime as well as the space component by dividing time into periods. He called each period a "day" (in Hebrew, "*yom*"). "There was evening and there was morning—the first day" (Genesis 1:5b). We must recognize the same Hebrew word *yom* is used in the latter part of this verse that was used in the first part of the verse where God contrasted the period of light with the period of darkness. This usage of "day" as opposed to "night" causes us no problem in understanding since we still use our word "day" in the same manner. Moreover, in Hebrew as in English, the word "day" can have several other meanings, and the appropriate meaning must always be determined based on the context.[9] Consequently, we must be careful with the second use of *yom* in verse 5. How should it be understood?

The second use of the word *yom* describes "an evening and a morning" period as being one "day." Using the word "morning" to indicate the coming of light and the word "evening" to indicate the end of the period of light and the coming of darkness are common usages throughout the Bible, as well as in speech today. Placing "evening" before "morning" in describing a "day" is in complete harmony with the instructions concerning the celebration of holy days that the LORD gave Moses, e.g., "It is a sabbath of complete rest for you. You shall humble yourselves on the ninth day of the month at evening. From that evening until the next evening, you shall observe a sabbath rest" (Leviticus 23:32). Consequently, there is no *a priori* reason to adopt any other meaning for the word *yom* than the one that we gain from a literal reading of

---

[8] God did not give entities names like "day" and "night" for his benefit but for the benefit of the readers so that they could clearly identify and differentiate among objects that had critical importance in his creation.

[9] Siegbert Becker, "Evolution and Genesis," *Wisconsin Lutheran Quarterly*, Vol. 75, No. 2 (April 1978), pp. 83-97.

Genesis 1:5, or of any of the verses in Genesis 1, namely, one terrestrial day. This is consistent with Exodus 20:11 and Exodus 31:17 where the LORD himself, in speaking to the people of Israel and to Moses, firmly asserted that He created the world in "six days." The worship life God mandated for Israel has many references to six workdays followed by a day of rest, corresponding to the period of creation (e.g., Exodus 16:26). There is no textual reason to consider any other meaning of the second *yom* than that of a terrestrial day. Efforts by some to lengthen the days of Genesis into long periods of time have no scriptural support. They will be discussed in chapter 13 to show the problem inherent in them.

God's First Separation of Materials

By the second period of creation, God had established the pattern of separating his creative acts by a unit called "day." The day was an evening and a morning, i.e., a period of inaction and a period of activity. On the second day, God began sorting and separating the materials that he had created on the first day. "God said, 'Let there be an expanse between the waters, and let it separate the water from the water'" (Genesis 1:6). The mention of water gives us important information concerning the nature of the physical components that God made when he called the universe into existence. This created material might have been anything from a superheated plasma made up of subatomic particles, like the interior of the sun, to the superdense material of a neutron star, to a frozen mass near absolute zero, like the moons of the outer planets of the solar system. We would have no ability to know what the created world was like at this point if it were not for the mention of water. Water is a moleculear substance composed of atoms, so the Earth was not like a plasma or a neutron star. It was composed of molecules and apparently a mixture of water and solid materials. That the word "water" is used and not "ice" or "steam" gives us a clue to the apparent temperature of the world, but we should not try to push our reasoning any further. We need additional revelation before we can deduce more. This intervention by God had the effect of separating the surface of the planet Earth from the rest of the watery mass.

Having called into existence an "expanse" to separate the available water into two bodies, God then tailored the expanse to accomplish the separation. "God made the expanse, and he separated the water that was below the expanse from the water that was above the expanse, and it was so. God called the expanse 'sky'" (Genesis 1:7,8a). This part of God's creative work seems clear and understandable, but it raises questions in our curious minds. For example, what happened to the water God placed above the sky? Did it merely become the clouds? Was it used to regulate the Earth's climate from this elevated position before the flood? Was it referred to again when "the floodgates of the sky were opened" (Genesis 7:11)? We do not know, nor can we find, the answers to these questions. We can speculate about them, but that carries with it the risk that we will form in our minds additions to what was revealed in the Bible and thus be led to rely on our own wisdom in judging the things of God.

This part of the Genesis account opens the door to an even more fundamental question, "What is the sky?" Is it the lowest tier of the three-tiered view of heaven that ancient peoples held? Or did God create the sky as some sort of barrier that existed around the Earth before the flood? If we look up today when it is clear, we can see an apparent layer of blue above us. This, however, is an illusion caused by sunlight being refracted by the Earth's atmosphere. This is not what would have been seen at the end of the second day of creation because the sun did not yet exist. Would an observer at the end of the sixth day have seen the same thing we see when we look upward today? We do not know.

As we proceed with the Genesis account, we must be aware of a general principle of biblical interpretation. In the Bible, God frequently described things using the reference points that were known to the people at the time when a particular part of the Scriptures was written. Moses wrote Genesis under God's inspiration so it would have made sense to, and contained useful information for, the people 1400 years before Christ. We must be careful not to use our greater understanding of the physical world to try to box God in with our view of reality. On the other hand, we do know certain creative acts described in the Bible required other creative acts, which are not mentioned, to be carried out. These will be discussed as they are encountered.

The second day ended as did the first, with a barren planet, but a planet in a greater state of organization. The Bible reports, "There was evening and there was morning—the second day" (Genesis 1:8b). While the second day may have seemed like an easy day for God, we do not know what else he might have done that was not recorded. The Earth has a complex structure, and whether he did organizational work on this structure on the second day, we have no way of discerning. Explanations of such structural work would have had little meaning to the people at the time of Moses, so including any details about such actions by God might only have confused the early readers. This is an important constraint that should be kept in mind whenever details that we would love to know are not provided. We should be careful that our curiosity does not lead us astray as it did Eve. Nevertheless, we should be aware as we study the rest of Genesis 1 in the following chapter that the conditions on the Earth that were needed to support fully developed living things involved more than inert ground and water. There had to be an atmosphere, rich soil, and means to protect living things from the destructive radiation of the sun. That God did not reveal all his creative acts in relation to these things does not mean that he did not perform such acts. In the words of Jesus, "So do not worry about tomorrow, for tomorrow will care for itself. Each day has enough trouble of its own" (Matthew 6:34). If we should not worry about God taking care of us in the future, how much less should we worry about how he worked in the past to give us what we have today!

The end of the second day of terrestrial history is a good place to end this chapter. The groundwork was moving along nicely, and it would soon be ready for the introduction of living creatures. The next four days would radically change the appearance of the planet.

4

Populating the Creation

The light returned to the barren Earth. It was the third day in the world's history, and it would be an eventful day in God's creative process. It was the day on which the LORD separated the land from the seas and introduced physical life into his creation.

God's Second Separation of Materials

God began the third day by making major geological changes to the underlying planet that he had created. Before this point in time, the land might have simply been covered with the water or the land and the water might have been totally entangled in a murky mixture. We do not know how they were organized, but we do know that God acted. "God said, 'Let the waters under the sky be gathered together to one place, and let the dry land appear,' and it was so. The waters under the sky gathered to their own places, and the dry land appeared" (Genesis 1:9). God spoke, and suddenly the situation was very different. What happened needs some consideration.

Using numerous methods of investigation, geologists have developed a model of the structure of planet Earth as it currently exists. The model has a core and various layers that explain what we observe, such as the Earth's magnetic field and the existence of volcanoes.[1] However, we do not know, and it is truly unimportant, what the underlying structure of the mass that constituted God's creation was during the first two days. Any turbulence due to natural forces that might have occurred could easily have been rectified by God's restructuring of the planet on the third day. This situation in which any signi-

---

[1] John J. Renton, *The Nature of Earth: An Introduction to Geology*, The Great Courses (Chantilly, Virginia: The Teaching Company, 2006).

ficant internal changes to the Earth were irrelevant needed to be dramatically altered as God approached his act of creating living things. Living things require a stable environment. If the planet were to irregularly convulse or haphazardly change its physical structure, it would not be a perfect, or perhaps not even a possible, environment for plant life to flourish. Given that God's standard is perfection,[2] we would expect God at some point to have established a stable environment. We know he did, because we see such a generally stable environment on the earth today, although its quality has been significantly compromised by sin.

To cause the water existing below the sky to move to specific places and to stay there, God shaped the solid components of his creation, such as rocks, cobble, sand, and dirt, so that these divergent materials would firmly cling together. The Bible does not mention a separate event in which God created gravity, but the creation of what non-scientists commonly call "the force of gravity" was essential for holding the components of the ground together.[3] God placed some portions of the ground farther from the center of the earth than other portions, allowing gravity to act as his servant to cause the water to obey his command and to be collected in the lowest places available. Today we know that gravity not only causes the seas to remain in "their own place" but also causes all manner of objects to remain on the earth's surface.

After God separated the ground from the water, he named these two components, as he had previously named the light and the darkness, to make the account of creation more understandable to the readers. "God called the dry ground 'land,' and the gathering places of the waters he called 'seas'" (Genesis 1:10a). With this major reshaping of the planet complete, God reviewed his work and was satisfied.[4] "God saw that it was good" (Genesis 1:10b).

---

[2] He is the Rock! Perfect is his work. Indeed all of his ways are justice. He is a faithful God. He does no wrong. Righteous and upright is he. (Deuteronomy 32:4)

[3] Today our best scientific model of gravity is that space itself is curved by the presence of matter, but the effects are nearly the same as those predicted by Newton's laws of motion in most cases. See Benjamin Schumacher, *Black Holes, Tides, and Curved Spacetime: Understanding Gravity*, The Great Courses (Chantilly, Virginia: The Teaching Company, 2013), Lectures 14-17.

[4] God, of course, does not need to inspect his work as a craftsman or a project foreman might to make sure nothing was missed or had been mishandled in the implementation of the project. This statement appears for the benefit of the readers to remind them that God leaves nothing to chance in his creation and management of the world.

The Creation of Plant Life

Let us first consider the simplicity of the biblical description of God's creation of plant life, and then let us investigate the complicated environment that God had to establish in the process of creating these living things. As before, God created merely by speaking. "God said, 'Let the earth produce plants—vegetation that produces seed, and trees that bear fruit with its seed in it—each according to its own kind on the earth,' and it was so" (Genesis 1:11). Naturally, the earth responded to its creator's command without hesitation. "The earth brought forth plants, vegetation that produces seed according to its own kind, and trees that bear fruit with its seed in it, each according to its own kind, and God saw that it was good" (Genesis 1:12). The dry land established earlier in the day produced plants and presumably so did the bottoms of the seas and of the lakes because we find plants on the bottoms of these bodies of water today. Some of this created vegetation was of substantial size (e.g., large trees).

We know from our own efforts at gardening that plants do not grow on barren rocks or in sand. They require soil that has nutrients the plants can extract to grow stems, leaves, and flowers. Soil gets the nutrients it contains from the decay of dead plants and animals and from the waste products of animals. Yet, before the third day there were no plants and animals to die and decay. A soil so rich in nutrients that it could sustain numerous large and small plants, and even a lush garden (Genesis 2:8-14), had to be part of God's creative process for plants. In other words, when God created the soil on the third day, he had to have given it an apparent age of thousands of years, the length of time that would have been required for it to develop through natural processses.[5] Had soil scientists examined it on that day, this would have been their conclusion concerning the age of the soil. In other words, the real age of the soil was only minutes old, but its apparent age was thousands of years old.

This situation opens the door to the important issue of how we determine the age of any object.[6] If we saw an artist complete a painting two days ago, the painting would be two days old. If, however, the painting was a copy of

---

[5] Arthur A. Eggert and Geoffrey A. Kieta, *Clearing a Path for the Gospel* (Sun Prairie, Wisconsin: In Terra Pax Lutheran Publishing, 2019), pp. 110-114.

[6] Paul Boehlke, "Contemplating Our Navels: Consideration of Time That Never Was," *Charis*, Vol. 4 (Lent 2005), pp. 23-29.

another that was painted 400 years ago and if the artist had copied the style exactly, many people would be deceived into believing the new painting was really 400 years old. Two days would be the "actual age," but 400 years would be the "apparent age."[7] Even experts have been fooled into believing recent copies of older paintings are the real thing. This is the analogous situation that we are seeing when examining the soil that supported the vegetation on the third day. Soil scientists, using the available instrumentation and their experience, would have given a completely wrong answer because they would not have considered the possibility of supernatural intervention in the locale where their examinations were being made. This introduces a limitation of science that we will explore in chapter 11.

Soil was not the only physical issue that God had to address in his creation of plants. Plants depend on the atmosphere for raw materials for their biochemical reactions, for bulk moisture in the form of dew and rain, and for protection against the ultraviolet radiation of the sun. The development of an atmosphere is an extremely complex procedure. An oxygen-rich atmosphere reacts with everything it touches, and it touches nearly everything. This causes the amount of atmospheric oxygen to rapidly decline if it is not continually replenished. For an oxygen-rich atmosphere to be built, oxygen would have to be generated by plants faster than it disappears through numerous common reactions. A comparison of the atmosphere of the Earth with that of Venus, often called Earth's twin sister, illustrates the problem. The composition of Earth's atmosphere is 20.9% oxygen, 78% nitrogen, 0.04% carbon dioxide and 1% argon,[8] while the composition of Venus' atmosphere is 96.5% carbon dioxide, 3.5% nitrogen and 0.00% oxygen. Being 90 times as dense as that of the Earth's atmosphere, Venus' atmosphere is crushingly heavy, and its temperature is 860° Fahrenheit.[9] Yet, Venus is the same physical size as the Earth. Because the amount of oxygen in the Earth's atmosphere is very hard to maintain, it is estimated it would have taken several hundred million years of progressive plant evolutionary history to change a carbon dioxide-rich atmosphere into the type of atmosphere that is found on Earth today. God created this atmosphere on the second or third day of the first week to sustain the

---

[7] The "actual age" of something is the amount of time that has elapsed since it was created. Its "apparent age" is how old it appears to our senses or our instrumentation. People normally say "age" whether they mean "actual age" or "apparent age." We must determine their meaning from the context of the statement. These two ages are not always the same.
[8] *Earth* (Wikipedia, Online Encyclopedia).
[9] *Venus* (Wikipedia, Online Encyclopedia).

plants he created, even though he gave it an apparent age of several hundred million years at its creation.

Plants can live in atmospheres of lower quality than animals, but larger plants still need a substantial amount of support from a plant-friendly environment. Rain, the major source of moisture for the earth, can be a tricky matter.[10] There must be enough water vapor entering the atmosphere to provide the aqueous substance for rain, but there must also be favorable air currents and the presence of various triggers to cause the rain to fall in specific places. The existence of vast deserts on Earth is evidence of the complexity of rainfall developing. Moreover, an atmosphere suitable for sustaining life must provide protection against the destructive parts of the solar radiation spectrum. Radiation of some wavelengths can destroy molecules by rupturing their chemical bonds, causing the molecules containing those bonds to come apart and re-form into non-useful, and even harmful, new molecules. Since the sun was not yet in existence on the third day in Genesis 1, the light created on the first day may not have posed the same problem as sunlight does. However, by the end of the fourth day, a protective mechanism in the Earth's atmosphere against harmful radiation needed to be in place.[11] Today, an ozone layer serves that purpose, but it would have taken at least several hundred years to develop by natural processes. Divine creation was therefore involved in some manner.

The Bible never mentions the creation of microorganisms, that is, organisms that cannot be seen with the naked eye. A microscope is required to view them, and they might be composed of one or numerous cells. Some microorganisms are plant-like and can capture and store the energy of the sun through photosynthesis or through chemosynthesis. Most are more similar to animals, consuming other microorganisms to gain the energy to live and reproduce. The number of different species and subspecies of microorganisms is unknown, but current estimates run from ten million up to one trillion.[12] These organisms are present in large numbers (i.e., millions or billions)

---

[10] Eric R. Snodgrass, *The Science of Extreme Weather*, The Great Courses (Chantilly, Virginia: The Teaching Company, 2016).

[11] The sun has a characteristic spectrum of radiation based on the physics by which radiation is produced within the sun. While God certainly could have changed the way the sun operated after the fall, such dramatic reengineering of the laws of physics in the universe seems incompatible with the creation being completed by the end of the sixth day.

[12] "Researchers find that Earth may be home to 1 trillion species," News Release 16-052 (Washington, DC: National Science Foundation, 2016).

literally everywhere, and they are involved in the great majority of living processes in some way. An average human body may contain almost as many bacterial (non-human) cells as human cells.[13] Their presence is essential to plant life,[14] so the evidence strongly indicates that God made many bacterial species when he created plants.

Finally, it is of great theological significance that God created plants before he created the sun, which today is the source of energy for all plant and animal life. This shows the LORD is capable of sustaining life directly by his almighty power, without the usual natural means. Therefore, we dare not try to bind God's hands by restricting him to working through the laws of nature. Certainly, plant life could not have survived for any significant amount of time without either sunlight or without God's direct sustaining effort. Because neither lack of sunlight nor divine intervention is consistent with evolutionary models, the third period of creation cannot be stretched from a single day to millions of years to meet an evolutionary timeline.[15] That would be incompatible with God's revelation concerning his creating activity.

When we consider all the support mechanisms that God needed to put in place to create and sustain plant life, we realize just how momentous the third day of creation truly was. Nevertheless, God restricted the biblical description to only four verses. God does not need to brag about his accomplishments. He is! And he is almighty! And we cannot even imagine his power. He concludes his revelation of the third day as he did the previous two. "There was evening and there was morning—the third day" (Genesis 1:13).

The "Second Heaven"

As described in a chapter 2 footnote, ancient peoples believed there were three levels of heaven. Because this was how the first readers would have un-

---

[13] At one point it was thought that 90% of the cells in humans were bacteria, but this was shown to be false. (A Abbott. "Scientists bust myth that our bodies have more bacteria than human cells." *Nature* (2016). https://doi.org/10.1038/nature.2016.19136)

[14] Plants need nitrogen to make amino acids but cannot take nitrogen from the air because they have no biological pathway to do so. Certain bacteria form symbiotic relationships with the roots of particular plants and convert atmospheric nitrogen into nitrogen compounds in the soil that plants can then absorb. Plants requires these bacteria to survive. See Kevin Ahern, *Biochemistry and Molecular Biology*, The Great Courses (Chantilly, Virginia: The Teaching Company, 2019), Lecture 19.

[15] "Evolution" simply means change. Almost everything changes, so almost everything evolves. As used in this book, "evolution" will mean "large-scale evolution" that produces dramatic changes in plant and animal species, or in the environment of the Earth.

Populating the Creation

derstood the account, we need to consider the Bible's revelation in view of this model. God created the components of the lowest level of heaven (i.e., the "first" heaven) by the end of the third day. Thus, God established the "first heaven," i.e., the atmosphere, because it was essential for life to exist on the Earth. Having produced what was of immediate concern, on the fourth day God turned his attention to the space above the atmosphere, the so-called "second heaven," namely, what we often refer to as "outer space." Once again, what God reveals to us in the Scriptures is simply stated, but its implications are monumental.

"God said, 'Let there be lights in the expanse of the sky to divide the day from the night, and let them serve as markers to indicate seasons, days, and years'" (Genesis 1:14). Before revealing the nature of the "lights" he commanded to appear in the sky, God tells us why they were being placed there. They would be involved in the separation between day and night that he had previously established. They would also be markers for time intervals not previously introduced, namely, "seasons" and "years." God had all these things planned from eternity, even though seasons and years were things still to come in the future.

God also designed his newly created objects to have the ability and the responsibility for lighting the Earth. God would henceforth routinely work through such means as his agents rather than through direct use of his almighty power to provide the light that the earth required. God continued speaking, "'Let them serve as lights in the expanse of the sky to give light to the earth,' and it was so" (Genesis 1:15). Giving light was the second purpose for which they were created.

In only a few words the Bible then disclosed what God had created, "God made the two great lights: the greater light to rule the day, and the lesser light to rule the night. He also made the stars" (Genesis 1:16). God did not think it necessary to name these objects, as he had named some objects previously, or to explain how they would rule the day and the night. We can easily deduce the greater light is the sun, and when the sun is above the horizon, it sets the tone for what is observed in the sky. The sky is bright, and we have difficulty seeing other objects in it. Even when the sky is overcast, the solar radiation almost always brightens the atmosphere. The moon, on the other hand, has a much weaker rule over the night. Even on cloudless nights, there are times when it is not seen in the sky at all or is only extant as a narrow crescent.

Cloud cover may obscure its presence completely. While the light of the moon exceeds the light of the stars when it is present, the total amount of light it provides on even the brightest night is but a small fraction of the light available in the daytime. Although God did choose to give some light to the earth at night, his primary light source was placed in what he called "day." Before considering the challenging details of the fourth day, let us note God's recap of his activities. "God set these lights in place in the expanse of the sky to provide light for the Earth, to rule over the day and over the night, and to divide the light from the darkness. God saw that it was good" (Genesis 1:17,18).

We realize how little God has told us about his creation and about his handling of the celestial bodies when we recognize that he did not reveal to us that he placed the earth into orbit around the sun. Nor did he mention that he made the earth to rotate on its axis to cause the pattern of light and darkness that we observe. There was initially no easy way for people to determine this information from observing the sky. They therefore concluded all celestial objects orbited the earth, and they read confirmation for that view into the account of the fourth day of creation. That people assumed the earth was stationary and everything orbited it was not of particular importance to daily life in the past, and it is still not very important for most people today. The difficulty with the idea of a geocentric solar system is not that it led to people making foolish life decisions, but that people tried to explain the movements in the heavens based on their misinterpretation of the Bible rather than based on observations of the physical world. God did not say in Genesis or elsewhere in the Scriptures that all celestial objects orbited the earth. People, nevertheless, made the false assumption that everything they observed in the world had to have some explanation in the Bible. Celestial objects seemed to them to orbit the earth, and God created these objects after he created the earth, so they drew a logical but a false conclusion. Worse yet, they persecuted people who did not understand this part of the Scriptures the same way they did. This should serve as a warning not to read into the Bible what we think ought to be there.[16]

The sun was a brand-new object on the fourth day, yet like the soil and the atmosphere, it had a much greater apparent age. We know today that the nuclear reactions in the center of the sun, which is an extremely hot plasma, generates radiation by fusion over a large portion of the electromagnetic spectrum

---

[16] Every word of God has been refined. He is a shield to those who take refuge in him. Do not add to his words. If you do, he will correct you, and you will be shown to be a liar. (Proverbs 30:5-6)

Populating the Creation 43

(including visible light).[17] One measure of the age of the sun is the length of time that it took for the first light generated in the core of the sun to reach its surface and be radiated. Due to the tremendous density of material in the center of the sun, a light photon (i.e., the particle associated with a light wave) travels an incredibly short distance before it is absorbed by some nuclear particle. It then is reradiated, reabsorbed, reradiated, etc. through innumerable cycles before reaching the solar surface. Because of the sun's size, this process would take several thousand years. As a result, the surface of the sun would have been dark for at least several millennia after God created it on the fourth day if he had not also created the sun with sufficient apparent age that its surface had reached a steady state of light emission. A more accurate measurement of the apparent solar age can be made based on the fraction of its hydrogen fuel that the sun has apparently already consumed and how rapidly it is consuming that fuel. The information necessary to draw conclusions is obtained by analyzing the strength of the emission spectra of the materials making up the sun. Based on these measurements, it appears the sun has been burning fuel for about 5 billion years. This means God gave the sun a very old apparent age when he created it. While someday other measuring approaches may cause scientists to refine their estimate of the apparent age of the sun, that apparent age will still be very much older than its actual age, which is the time that has elapsed since God created it. God has his purposes both for creating objects with large specific apparent ages and for not telling us why. We need to trust God so we do not question him or try to explain to him how he must have done it.

Because the moon is not a primary light source, as it only reflects sunlight, its age cannot be measured in the same manner. If we look at the moon, however, even with a moderate-power telescope, we see a highly pitted surface consistent with the moon having been bombarded with meteors over many, many years and with it having had a more malleable surface during some period in the past. At the rate that meteors enter the Earth/moon system, it would have taken many million years for the moon to have acquired as many craters as we observe on it today. Even without using more sophisticated

---

[17] Alex Filippenko, *Understanding the Universe: Introduction to Astronomy*, 2nd ed., The Great Courses (Chantilly, Virginia: The Teaching Company, 2007), Lecture 27.

measuring techniques, it is evident that the LORD also created the moon with a significant apparent age.

The stars present an even more challenging situation due to the restricted ability scientists possess to study them. The Earth receives radiation from outside the solar system over the entire electromagnetic spectrum from gamma rays to radio waves. In addition, there are the rare celestial events that cause neutrino bursts and huge gravitational waves, but these two phenomena are extremely difficult to detect and measure. Although scientists have collected enormous quantities of data, they are limited to making long-distance observations of the objects that are outside the solar system. The great distances to even the nearest stars, which would take centuries to traverse with current technology, prevent us from using probes productively to study the stars, as we have used them to study the planets and moons within the inner solar system. What is certain is that the values for the stellar distances that have been computed by the best available techniques are incompatible with the stars having been visible from Earth immediately after their creation if only natural processes had been involved in the propagation of their light. It would have taken more than four years for the nearest star to appear in the night sky, and additional stars would have been gradually popping up in the sky ever since as their light finally reached the Earth. Today many of the features that we can easily see in the night sky would still be lacking if their light had left them on the first day of their divine creation. This forces us to conclude that the LORD not only created the sources of stellar radiation, but he also created the light rays between all those sources and the Earth so that the stars could immediately be seen.

The conclusion we have just been forced to draw opens the door to another possibility—did God create the stars as burning "suns" in distant places in the heavens or did he merely create the light that apparently comes from them? The Scriptures never state that the stars are sun-like spheres, even though this is a reasonable conclusion to draw from the observations that people have made of the heavens.[18] We need to recall that on the first day God created light without a physical source. On the fourth day he created light rays that

---

[18] We must be careful here not to say too much because the Genesis account makes a distinction between light in Genesis 1:3-5 and "light-bearers" or "luminaries" in Genesis 1:14-16. While the latter verses use "luminaries" only to describe the sun and the moon and not to describe the stars, it is clear Moses is making a distinction between light per se and the objects that bear light (also see Ezekiel 32:7-8).

Populating the Creation

only appeared to come from the surface of stars. Jesus told his followers that "the stars will fall from the sky" (Matthew 24:29), which could not literally happen if they were objects of the size of the sun or many times larger.[19] The astronomical model seems very plausible, but unless and until we can probe the universe at large, there is no way of telling what is physically on the created stage of the universe and what is merely on a sophisticated backdrop of created light rays. Both possibilities would produce exactly what we can see with our eyes and detect with our instruments.

The myriad different phenomena that scientists have observed in the sky is mind-boggling. Whether God created what the scientists conclude they are observing or whether the starry host is merely an example of God's special effects for man's benefit, studying astronomy and astrophysics greatly expands our idea of what God's being "almighty" really means. Imagine all this grandeur packed into the short sentence "He also made the stars" (Genesis 1:16b).

The Bible concludes the narrative of the fourth day as it did the first three. "There was evening and there was morning—the fourth day" (Genesis 1:19). The key points for us to remember are that the universe has an apparent age of at least several billion years and that God did not record most of what he did in his creation process on the fourth day for us to read and contemplate.

The Fifth Day

During the first four days God created objects that stayed where they were placed (e.g., rocks, flowers) or that moved in set patterns (e.g., the sun, the moon). On the fifth day the LORD created entities capable of movement based on their own desires and instincts. This included numerous types of sea creatures and multiple types of winged creatures. "God said, 'Let the waters swarm with living creatures, and let birds and other winged creatures fly above the earth in the open expanse of the sky'" (Genesis 1:20). These creatures were commanded to increase in number and to populate the sea and the land, each according to its "kind." "God created the large sea creatures and every living creature that moves, with which the waters swarm, according to

---

[19] The volume of the sun is about a million times that of the earth.

their own kind, and every winged bird according to its own kind" (Genesis 1:21a).

To the people who first read or heard these words, the message they conveyed was reassuring. When two similar animals mated, they would produce young animals that were like them. Salmon would mate to produce salmon, eagles would mate to produce eagles, and doves would mate to produce doves. Strange creatures would not be produced by the mating of common animals. They could trust that God's creation was governed by reliable laws both for inert physical objects and for living things.

The situation is less straightforward for us today because we know much more about how animals and plants breed and how that breeding is controlled by genetics. We know that there are millions of animal species today and that some of them appear remarkably similar to each other when viewed by the casual observer. The number of species far exceeds what a human could identify and name in many years, much less in a fraction of a day as Adam did on the sixth day of creation (Genesis 2:19). This leads to an issue that must be considered. The Bible does not tell us whether "kind" is a generalization, such as "waterfowl," or a very specific designation, such as "mallard duck." Prior to the era of genetic knowledge, it was common to say that small variations, such as color, might have occurred since the creation but to firmly insist that "a duck is a duck and always was a duck."[20] Today we know things that look very different can have the same genetic code (e.g., a caterpillar and a butterfly are genetically identical), while other animals that appear quite similar are genetically very different (e.g., rabbits and hares do not even have the same number of chromosomes). The question "What is a kind?" applies to plants as well as to all the animals created on the fifth and sixth days. Because the Bible does not define "kind," we dare not do so either, because we do not have divine revelation to further clarify the definition. Similarly, just because St. Paul wrote, "Flesh is not all the same kind. Instead, people have one kind of flesh, animals have another kind, birds another, and fish yet another" (1 Corinthians 15:39), we should not conclude that God divided living things into only four kinds at creation. More will be discussed about this in subsequent chapters.

God concluded his creation on the fifth day with an assessment and a blessing. "God saw that it was good. God blessed them when he said, 'Be fruitful

---

[20] Carl Lawrenz, "God's Unique Judgement of The Flood," *Wisconsin Lutheran Quarterly*, Vol. 71, No. 4 (October 1974), p. 275.

Populating the Creation

and multiply. Fill the waters of the seas, and let birds multiply on the earth'" (Genesis 1:21b,22). God's assessment told him the same thing his assessments had on previous days; he was creating a good universe and filling it with good creatures. God, moreover, did what he could not previously have done; he directly addressed other living beings. The objects of his creation on the fifth day were different from his previously created objects because they could choose, at least to some extent, how to behave and how to live their lives. God instructed them to multiply in number. From the limited number he created directly, they were to procreate more of the same "kind." While they could not create their offspring out of nothing as God had created them, their bodies could create them out of the materials in their environment according to the manner God had provided for them. Their descendants would be a blessing from God.

The fifth day closed as had each of the previous days with the simple statement, "There was evening and there was morning—the fifth day" (Genesis 1:23).

The Sixth Day

On the sixth day God completed his creation of the world. He had previously created plants, sea creatures, and creatures that flew through the atmosphere. It was now time for him to populate the surface of the planet itself. "God said, 'Let the earth produce living creatures according to their own kind, livestock, creeping things, and wild animals according to their own kind,' and it was so. God made the wild animals according to their own kind, and the livestock according to their own kind, and everything that creeps on the ground according to its own kind. God saw that it was good" (Genesis 1:24,25). As he had on the past days, the LORD separated what he had created into categories. Once again, he used the word "kind" to group the animals that he created, but also again, he used that word in such a manner that we cannot ascertain what he included within any particular "kind." God's work continued to be impressive, and he was satisfied with it.

At this point we will take a detour in our study of God's creation. God was about to create his special creature man. Due to the importance of man as the purpose of God's creation, chapter 6 will be dedicated to man's creation and to his interaction with God. In that chapter we will return to Genesis 1:26-29, as well as considering Genesis 2 and 3. Meanwhile, we will look at God's treatment of his non-human creation in the rest of Genesis 1.

The plants that God created on the third day could live directly from the nutrients in the soil and in the atmosphere. We already pondered how important it had been that God put these things into his creation even though he did not tell us he had done so. Once the sun was in place in the sky and God had provided a shield against its harmful radiation, the plants had what they needed to survive under God's protective care and command. The animals, on the other hand, could not eat dirt or live simply by breathing air. They needed real food, and God provided it. "'To every animal of the earth, and to every bird of the sky, and to everything that creeps on the earth, in which there is the breath of life, I have given every green plant for food.' And it was so" (Genesis 1:30).

God here made a clear distinction between animal life and plant life. While plants live and propagate, God declared that their deaths, which certainly occurred when they were eaten, were compatible with his creation being perfect.[21] They were expendable. While bacteria are not mentioned in the creation account, we have noted their presence was essential to the survival of larger living creatures. They also died as part of the purpose of their existence to support larger life forms. In addition, their death and digestion were important in maintaining the quality of the soil.

God instructed all of the animals he had created on days five and six to be herbivores. Because many animals are not herbivores today, we will need to again consider this matter when God intervened in his creation after man's fall into sin. At the creation, however, God made animal life sacred. Neither man nor animals had the right to take the life of any animal. Furthermore, due to God's command, animals were incapable of killing other animals because they did not have free will,[22] which would have permitted them to resist their maker.

---

[21] Plants and animals seem very different in their physical characteristics and in their behaviors, and they are treated very differently in the Bible. Nevertheless, their underlying genetics are the same. Both plant and animal DNA codes protein synthesis in the same way, using sequential sets of three consecutive bases on the primary DNA strand to specify the order in which to insert amino acids from the group of the 20 amino acids that are common to all life forms. Often the proteins are very similar or identical among various species of plants and animals. God's distinction between plants and animals was based solely on his will, not on any fundamental differences that he placed in their life processes. See Ahern, *Biochemistry*, Lecture 3.

[22] Free will is the ability to decide to follow God's will. Only man and the angels received it at their creation. The rebellious angels and man lost it when they sinned, and the "holy" an-

The end of God's six days of creation had been reached. It was time for a final assessment at the conclusion to his work. "God saw everything that he had made, and indeed, it was very good. There was evening and there was morning—the sixth day" (Genesis 1:31).

The actions of God during creation week are far beyond our ability to comprehend. We have looked at some of the implications of the simple words of the text, and we have realized that in his creating activities, God did much more than he directly revealed to us. We have attempted to fill in the gaps based on what we know about how natural processes work—such as plants' need for nutrients in the soil, such as a breathable atmosphere that is essential to most life but that is difficult to maintain, and such as the organization of the celestial bodies that cannot be directly deduced from how the creation is described. On the other hand, we have avoided speculating about how God might have done what he did or reading into the Scriptures conclusions that we were not forced to draw.

We will discover more about the divine creation in the next chapters because this story is far too big to be covered by 27 verses of biblical text. Our next goal will be to examine how God continued to reference and document his creative work throughout the Bible.

---

gels then had it removed from them by God. (see Lyle L. Luchterhand, *Man*, People's Bible Teaching series (Milwaukee: Northwestern Publishing House, 1998), pp. 65-66.)

5

Continuing Revelation on the Creation

Throughout the first chapter of the Holy Scriptures the LORD revealed his general creation to us in almost outline form. Some people find it easy to say this account was just a written record of ancient mythology that was thereafter allowed to fade into the background as later events took center stage and assumed a greater importance. Such a statement would be utterly false because references to and information about the creation account continue to appear throughout the Bible. Kings, prophets, apostles, priests, and Levites talked about God's general creative activities, and Jesus Christ himself used his ability as the Creator in his ministry. As we examine the passages of Scripture that reference the creation, we gain confidence in the importance that the LORD himself places on his creative acts.

Old Testament History

After the six days of creation, the LORD did something that at first seems incredible to us—he rested! The Bible relates, "The heavens and the earth were finished, along with everything in them. On the seventh day God had finished his work that he had done, and he rested on the seventh day from all his work that he had been doing" (Genesis 2:1-2). Certainly, the omnipotent God was not tired. He did not need to take a breather to prepare for his next project, nor was he intending to retire from being active and involved with his creation, as some seventeenth century philosophers (e.g., René Descartes, Isaac Newton, and Robert Boyle) thought he had. The LORD was instead setting an example for mankind. People were not to be so concerned with making their way in the world that they would work continually to get ahead. Already in the matter of the gift of manna, God showed he would provide enough in six days so that people did not have to work on the seventh day, the Sabbath. Moses said to the Israelites, "Six days you will gather it, but on the seventh day, the Sabbath, there will not be any" (Exodus 16:26). God had a different intention for the seventh day. The Bible records, "God blessed the seventh day and set it apart as holy, because on it he rested from all his work of creation that he had done" (Genesis 2:3). The seventh day was to be holy to the LORD so that the people would rest from their labors and seek their God.

After God had rescued his people from slavery in Egypt, he brought them to himself in a place of isolation. Speaking from Mount Sinai, the LORD himself said, "Remember the Sabbath day by setting it apart as holy. Six days you are to serve and do all your regular work, but the seventh day shall be a sabbath rest to the LORD your God. Do not do any regular work, neither you, nor your sons or daughters, nor your male or female servants, nor your cattle, nor the alien who is residing inside your gates, for in six days the LORD made the heavens and the earth, the sea, and everything that is in them, but he rested on the seventh day. In this way the LORD blessed the seventh day and made it holy" (Exodus 20:8-11). In this message God reaffirmed that he did indeed create the world in six days and that he had set aside the seventh day as a Sabbath, a day of rest.

God repeated both his claim of creating the world in six days and his demand that the people respect his desire concerning the Sabbath. The LORD said to Moses after he had called him up the mountain, "It [the Sabbath] is a permanent sign between me and the people of Israel, for in six days the LORD made heaven and earth, and on the seventh day he rested and was refreshed" (Exodus 31:17).

Moses later warned the people, "Beware so that you do not lift up your eyes to the heavens and see the sun and the moon and the stars, all the vast army of the heavens, and you are lured away, and you bow down to them and worship them—things that the LORD your God has allotted to all the nations under all the heavens" (Deuteronomy 4:19). The things of the heavens were the LORD's because he had created them; Israel's God was not a thief who stole what others had done. Later Moses again reminded the Israelites, "Indeed, the heavens and the heaven of heavens, the earth and everything that is on it—these belong to the LORD your God" (Deuteronomy 10:14). The Israelites were merely tenants for a time and stewards of the LORD's property, as are we. He is the creator and the owner.

As time passed, the Israelites often forgot from whom their blessings came, especially during the periods of the judges and of their later history. King David affirmed that he knew everything was from the LORD when he said, "But the LORD made the heavens" (1 Chronicles 16:26). Later, he glorified God, saying, "Blessed are you, LORD, the God of Israel, our father, from eternity to eternity. To you, O LORD, belong greatness, power, glory, victory, and majesty, because everything in the heavens and on the earth belongs to you" (1 Chronicles 29:10,11).

After Solomon succeeded David as king, Huram, the king of Tyre, said, "Blessed be the LORD, the God of Israel, who made the heavens and the earth" (2 Chronicles 2:12a). When he faced trouble, King Hezekiah of Judah prayed, "O LORD, God of Israel, you are seated above the cherubim. You alone are God over all the kingdoms of the earth. You made the heavens and the earth" (2 Kings 19:15). After the Jews' return from captivity, the Levite choir sang, "You made the heavens—the highest heavens and their entire army, the earth and everything that is on it, the seas and all that is in them" (Nehemiah 9:6).

This testimony concerning God's creation shows that it was accepted by leading men throughout Israel's history. As with all truths about God and his work, it was spoken under the influence of the Holy Spirit[1] and recorded at the direction of the Holy Spirit. In the words of St. Paul, "All Scripture is God breathed and is useful for teaching, for rebuking, for correcting, and for training in righteousness, so that the man of God may be complete, well equipped for every good work" (2 Timothy 3:16,17). God's creation was important, and throughout the history of Israel it was acknowledged, and God was praised for it.

The Wisdom Literature

In addition to the history books in the Old Testament, the LORD gave his people "wisdom literature" contained in five books that are structured very differently from each other—Job, Psalms, Proverbs, Ecclesiastes, and Song of Songs. These were intended to guide the behavior and worship of the Israelites. In the first three books, God's writers affirmed his general creation of the world, and we will consider what they wrote in this chapter. In the Psalms,

---

[1] Therefore I am informing you that no one speaking by God's Spirit says, "A curse be upon Jesus," and no one can say, "Jesus is Lord," except by the Holy Spirit. (1 Corinthians 12:3)

Proverbs, and Ecclesiastes, the LORD's penmen spoke concerning his creation of man, and those passages will be studied in chapter 6.

It was God himself who took the lead in avowing the claim that he was the great Creator. When he spoke directly to Job in Job chapters 38-41, he was emphatic about what he had done. He said, "Where were you when I laid the foundation of the earth?...Who determined its dimensions?...Who stretched out the surveying line over it? What supports its foundation? Who set its cornerstone in place?...Who locked up the sea behind doors when it burst out of the womb?...I [the LORD] said, 'You may come this far, but no farther. Here is the barrier for your proud waves.'...Have you ever set a time for the sun to rise?...Can you bind the chains of the Pleiades, or loosen the belt of Orion? Can you lead out the constellations at the right season and guide the Bear with her cubs? Do you know the laws that govern the skies? Can you establish God's rule on earth? Can you raise your voice to the clouds, so that a flood of water submerges you? Can you unleash the lightning bolts, so that they come and say to you, 'Here we are'?" (Job 38:4-35). In these selected verses from one of the four chapters, God clearly staked his claim to be the creator and manager of the world.

God inspired numerous psalmists to laud his creation and his ownership of the heavens and the earth. Ethan the Ezrahite wrote, "The heavens are yours, and yours also is the earth. You founded the world and everything that fills it. You created the north and the south. Tabor and Hermon shout for joy at your name. Your arm works for you with power. Your hand is strong. Your right hand is raised high" (Psalm 89:11-13). Another psalmist wrote, "Praise him, sun and moon. Praise him, all you bright stars. Praise him, you highest heavens and you waters which are above the heavens. Let them praise the name of the LORD, because he commanded, and they were created" (Psalm 148:3-5). Yet another wrote, "To him who alone does great wonders; To him who by his understanding made the heavens; To him who spread out the earth on the waters; To him who made the great lights, the sun to rule by day, the moon and stars to rule by night" (Psalm 136:4-9).[2] What the LORD did and his power to do it are acknowledged by these writers.

There are numerous additional verses in the psalms that recognize God as the "Maker" of the world and its contents. "For all the gods of the peoples are 'nothings,' but the LORD made the heavens" (Psalm 96:5). "May you be blessed by the LORD, the Maker of heaven and earth" (Psalm 115:15). "My

---

[2] Each line in this psalm ends with "For his mercy endures forever."

help comes from the LORD, the Maker of heaven and earth" (Psalm 121:2). "Our help is in the name of the LORD, the Maker of heaven and earth" (Psalm 124:8). "May the LORD, the Maker of heaven and earth, bless you from Zion" (Psalm 134:3). "His hope is in the LORD his God, the Maker of heaven and earth, the sea, and everything which is in them" (Psalm 146:5b,6a). The Book of Psalms was the hymnal of God's people Israel. Every time the Israelites sang these psalms, they confessed the LORD as the creator of the world. Clearly, God thought it important that they remember him as such.

Solomon wrote about the Wisdom of God and the creation, "The LORD possessed me at the beginning of his way, before his works of long ago.... before the origin of the earth. When there were no deep waters...when there were no springs filled with water. Before the mountains were settled in place, before the hills, I was brought forth, when he had not yet made land or fields or the first dust of the world. When he established the heavens....When he drew the horizon around the surface of the deep, when he placed the clouds in the sky above,...when he established his decree for the sea, so that the waters could not go beyond the limit set by his command, when he marked out the foundations of the earth" (Proverbs 8:22-29). We see in these selected verses that God, through Solomon, was telling of events in his initial creation.

The Prophets

The major prophets wrote about God as the creator of the physical universe, often emphasizing his almighty power. At a time when Israel had been taken into captivity and Judah was becoming apostate, Isaiah and Jeremiah tried to call the people back to the LORD, sometimes quoting God himself, by describing the reasons why their reliance had to be on him. For example, Isaiah quoted God, "To whom can you compare me as if we were equals? says the Holy One. Lift up your eyes to the heavens and see who created these things. See who brings out their army in great number and calls them all by name. Because of his great strength and mighty power, not one of them is missing" (Isaiah 40:25,26). Isaiah continued, "Do you not know? Have you not heard? The LORD is the eternal God. He is the Creator of the ends of the earth" (Isaiah 40:28a).

To strengthen his warning to Judah, sometimes Isaiah reminded the people that his message was coming from the mighty Creator God. "This is what the true God says, the LORD who creates the heavens and stretches them out, who spreads out the earth and everything that it produces" (Isaiah 42:5a). "This is what the LORD says. He created the heavens, He is God! He formed the earth and made it. Yes, he established it!" (Isaiah 45:18a). Other times he quoted a particular aspect of God's power. "I am the LORD, and there is no other. I am the one who forms light and creates darkness, the one who makes peace and creates disaster. I am the LORD, the one who does all these things" (Isaiah 45:6b,7). "This is what the LORD says, the Holy One of Israel, who formed Israel. Do you wish to question me concerning things to come? Will you give me orders about my children and about the work of my hands? I myself made the earth, and I created Adam upon it. With my hands I stretched out the heavens, and I commanded all their army" (Isaiah 45:11,12).

Above all, Isaiah wanted the people of Judah to understand they could not ignore the LORD with impunity. He warned them, "You have forgotten the LORD, your Creator, who stretches out the heavens, who makes the earth stand firm" (Isaiah 51:13). As a further reminder to these people, the Bible recorded for a second time the prayer of King Hezekiah when he was threatened by the king of Assyria. This prayer recognized that the "LORD of Armies, God of Israel" had "made the heavens and the earth" (Isaiah 37:16).

By the time of Jeremiah, the situation in Judah had reached the hopeless stage, but the LORD continued to remind the people through Jeremiah who he was and that he had the power to help them. Jeremiah quoted the LORD against the false gods and then explained, "'These gods, who did not make the heavens and the earth, will perish from the earth and from under the heavens.' But the one who made the earth by his power, established the world by his wisdom, and stretched out the heavens by his understanding—he thunders, and the waters in the heavens roar. He makes storm clouds rise from the ends of the earth. He makes lightning for the rain, and he brings out the wind from his warehouses" (Jeremiah 10:11b-13). Jeremiah continued that the LORD was not like the idols. "He who is the Portion of Jacob is not like these, because he is the Maker of all things (Jeremiah 10:16a).

As the time for the carrying out of the wrath of God upon Judah drew closer, Jeremiah continued his reminders about the God whom they were up against if they thought they could make their own way and worship idols. Jeremiah knew whom he himself worshipped when he wrote, "Ah, LORD God! You are the one who made the heavens and the earth by your great power and by your outstretched arm" (Jeremiah 32:17a). Concerning the idols he wrote, "He who is the Portion of Jacob is not like these, because he is the Maker of all things, including the tribe that is his possession. The LORD of Armies is his name" (Jeremiah 51:19). Sadly, Jeremiah's preaching fell on deaf ears because the people refused to recognize the LORD as the all-powerful Creator God.

The Gospels

In chapters 3 and 4 we saw God's creative power in terms of the natural world. Jesus, himself the Son of God, validated the truthfulness of the biblical account of that creative power by demonstrating his own command of the natural world. We will look at his actions in dealing with nature where no people were directly involved, so there can be no claim that his "apparent" miracles were aided by human collusion. Anytime God changed the course of nature merely with his word, we witness his creating power at work.

St. Matthew reported, "When he [Jesus] got into a boat, his disciples followed him. Suddenly a terrible storm came up on the sea, so that their boat was covered by the waves. But Jesus was sleeping....Then he got up, rebuked the wind and the sea, and there was a complete calm. The men were amazed, saying, "What kind of a man is this? Even the wind and the sea obey him!" (Matthew 8:23-27).

Once when Jesus wanted to go off alone to pray, his disciples tried to cross the Sea of Galilee. The boat began to be pounded by the waves. St. Matthew wrote, "In the fourth watch of the night, Jesus came toward them, walking on the sea. When the disciples saw him walking on the sea, they were terrified and cried out in fear, 'It's a ghost!'...When he got into the boat, the wind stopped. Those who were in the boat worshipped him, saying, 'Truly you are the Son of God!'" (Matthew 14:25-33). The wind and the sea recognized their Creator and obeyed him. The sea even allowed him to walk upon it as upon solid ground.

Twice when Jesus was in remote places, he created food to feed thousands of people. The first time, when he asked his disciples how much food they had, they told him, "five loaves and two fish." Then he "took the five loaves and the two fish. After looking up to heaven, he blessed them. He broke the loaves and gave them to the disciples. The disciples....picked up twelve basketfuls of what was left over from the broken pieces. Those who ate were about five thousand men, not even counting women and children" (Matthew 14:17-21). The second time there were "seven, and a few small fish." Jesus "took the seven loaves and the fish, gave thanks, and broke them. He gave them to the disciples, and the disciples gave them to the people....They picked up seven basketfuls of the broken pieces that were left over. Those who ate numbered four thousand men, without counting the women and children" (Matthew 15:34-38). For the Creator of the entire universe, adding a few thousand items of food to it was no challenge.

Jesus' acts involving nature were not limited to activities dealing with storms and bread. After Jesus was born, "Wise Men from the east came to Jerusalem. They asked, 'Where is he who has been born King of the Jews? We saw his star when it rose and have come to worship him'" (Matthew 2:1b,2). He created a new star or star pattern that influenced stargazers. At a wedding in Cana of Galilee, Jesus told the servants, "Fill the [six] jars with water." At Jesus' command they took some of this water to the master of the banquet, and the water had become fine wine. "The master of the banquet called the bridegroom and said to him, 'Everyone serves the good wine first, and when the guests have had plenty to drink, then the cheaper wine. You saved the good wine until now!'" (John 2:7-10). One morning sometime later Jesus himself was hungry. "Seeing a fig tree by the road, he went up to it but found nothing on it except leaves. He said to it, 'May there never be fruit from you again!' Immediately the fig tree withered away." (Matthew 21:19). Nothing can resist the word spoken by the eternal God.

Four other episodes provide strong demonstrations of Jesus' creating power as a member of the Godhead. St. John wrote, "In the beginning was the Word, and the Word was with God, and the Word was God. He was with God in the beginning. Through him everything was made, and without him not one thing was made that has been made." (John 1:1-3). St. John identified Jesus as the Creator God, present at the beginning. When talking with the religious leaders, Jesus identified himself as the eternal God. "Jesus said to them, 'Amen, Amen, I tell you: Before Abraham was born, I am'" (John 8:58). When he was crucified, he darkened the sun so it would not shine on him as he battled the powers of hell. "It was now about the sixth hour, and darkness came over the whole land until the ninth hour, while the sun was darkened. Then the curtain of the temple was torn in two" (Luke 23:44,45). Finally, after he had arisen victorious, locked doors and walls erected in the physical world could not prevent his passage through them. "On the evening of that first day of the week, the disciples were together behind locked doors because of their fear of the Jews. Jesus came, stood among them, and said to them, "Peace be with you!" After he said this, he showed them his hands and side. So the disciples rejoiced when they saw the Lord" (John 20:19,20).

From the molecules in a liquid to the bodies in the heavens, nothing could resist the word of the LORD when he spoke his commands. Everything adjusted itself to meet his pleasure, both during the first six days and when Jesus, God incarnate, walked upon the Earth.

The Apostles

To launch the Christian church, Jesus sent the Holy Spirit upon his chosen church leaders to give them the knowledge of the things of God that they were to proclaim to the world. These inspired men taught the divine creation in the same manner as had the prophets and the Scripture-writers of the Old Testament. The message of what God had done at creation had not become outdated or irrelevant.

The apostles confessed the LORD's creation of the world in various circumstances. For example, they included it in their praise of God for the release of St. Peter and St. John. "When they heard this, with one mind they raised their voices to God and said, 'Master, you are the God who made the heaven, the earth, the sea, and everything in them'" (Acts 4:24). They also referred to God's creation in their mission work. St. Paul and St. Barnabas said, "We are preaching the good news to you so that you turn from these worthless things to the living God, who made the heaven, the earth, the sea, and everything in them" (Acts 14:15b).

St. Paul included statements concerning God's creation in several of his epistles. To the Ephesians he wrote, "In past ages this mystery remained hidden in God, who created all things" (Ephesians 3:9b). In writing to the Colossians, he used the creation event to identify Jesus as true God. "He [Jesus] is the image of the invisible God, the firstborn over all creation, for in him all things were created, in heaven and on earth, things seen and unseen, whether thrones or dominions or rulers or authorities; all things have been created through him and for him. He is before all things, and all things hold together in him" (Colossians 1:15-17). St. Peter chastised the scoffers when he wrote, "You see, what they are intentionally forgetting is that the heavens came into existence long ago by the word of God and that the earth came together out of the water and between the waters" (2 Peter 3:5).

The writer to the Hebrews was "no nonsense" in his statement about the creation and how we are to know it is true. He wrote, "In the beginning, Lord, you laid the foundation of the earth, and the heavens are the works of your hands" (Hebrews 1:10b) and "By faith we know that the universe was created by God's word, so that what is seen did not come from visible things" (Hebrews 11:3). God created, he told us that he had created, and we are to believe it by faith, not by human proof.

Finally, in God's revelation to St. John, the theme of divine creation remains unchanged, even in the halls of heaven. The saints in glory sing, "Worthy are you, our Lord and God, to receive the glory and the honor and the power, for you have created all things, and because of your will they existed and were created" (Revelation 4:11). St. John wrote that the God of creation is the God by whom even the angels swear. "The angel whom I saw standing on the sea and on the land raised his right hand to heaven, and he swore by the one who lives forever and ever, who created the sky and the things in it, the earth and the things in it, and the sea and the things in it" (Revelation 10:5,6a).

From the first book of the Bible to its last book, the stated truth remained the same. God created the world in six days, and he alone deserves all glory for doing so. We are to acknowledge his creation and to praise him for it. Yet, we still have one more piece of the creation to examine, namely, the creation of the one living being on whose behalf all God's handiwork was performed. In chapter 6 we consider the creation of man.

6

Man – God's Special Creature

We have seen how the LORD created the universe and how he spoke about his creation often throughout the Scriptures, either through direct quotations or through his inspired writers. God's world was a marvelous place of perfect harmony, but we are naturally curious about why he created it. We need therefore to go back to Genesis 1 and consider God's creation of man, which, as we will learn, was the reason for God's great creation enterprise.

The Historical View of Man's Creation

When the rest of the creation had been completed, the time had come for God to add the crowning jewel to his work. "God said, 'Let us make man in our image, according to our likeness, and let them have dominion over the fish of the sea, and over the birds of the sky, and over the livestock, and over all the earth, and over every creeping thing that crawls on the earth'" (Genesis 1:26). This statement seems to imply that God at this instant in time had to take counsel within the Trinity to decide how he wanted to make man. It appears to be a last-minute decision. However, we must remember God is not a creature of time. The creation of man was part of God's Decree of Creation that happened in eternity. What we learn here is that there are multiple persons in the Godhead and that God did consider this monumental decision seriously.

As usual, God did what he had planned to do. "God created the man in his own image. In the image of God he created him. Male and female he created them" (Genesis 1:27). "So," we naturally ask, "what is the image of God?" Certainly, it could not have been that people looked like God to human eyes, because God is a spirit and has no physical body.[1] Pastor Lyle Luchterhand answered this question with the words, "The blessing of God's image was not merely that man was a superior rational being who could think and plan better than the animals but especially that man's intellect and will were rightly disposed toward God. Therefore, the image of God has sometimes been called the state of integrity or the state of innocence."[2] In other words, the image of God was not just that man could reason but that he knew God's will and was able to obey it perfectly.

Having created man as a rational being, God began to converse with his creature in a manner people then and now could understand. Mankind was assigned to be an agent of God. A major assignment given to mankind was to populate the earth. "God blessed them and said to them, 'Be fruitful, multiply, fill the earth, and subdue it'" (Genesis 1:28a). This was similar to the command to reproduce that God had given to the animals (Genesis 1:22), but having free will, mankind was capable of intellectually understanding and obeying this command as loving service to the LORD, unlike the animals that were simply bound to obey their creator.

God's next recorded command was for man to be God's agent in managing the earth. The command was directed to mankind, but it also was a command to all the creatures to be subject to man. God said, "Have dominion over the fish of the sea, over the birds of the sky, and over every living thing that moves on the earth" (Genesis 1:28b). Finally, God provided food for mankind by directing people to be vegetarians. "God said, 'Look, I have given you every plant that produces seed on the face of the whole earth, and every tree that bears fruit that produces seed. It will be your food'" (Genesis 1:29). With these words, God's historical account of man's creation was complete. However, God wanted us to know much more about his approach to the creation of man, and that information is contained in Genesis 2.

The Functional View of Man's Creation

Several people may view the same scene and see it totally differently. For example, a naturalist viewing a forested valley might see it in terms of the quality of habitat it offers woodland creatures. A lumberman viewing the

---

[1] [Jesus said,] "God is spirit, and those who worship him must worship in spirit and in truth." (John 4:24)

[2] Luchterhand, *Man*, pp. 56-57.
Koehler, *Christian Doctrine*, pp. 91-96.

Man – God's Special Creation

same forested valley might see it in terms of the number of board feet of quality lumber that could be harvested. The reports these observers would write would be quite different. What we remember or record about an event is often biased by our expectations of what we think will occur under the existing circumstances. At other times, two different accounts of an event can be intentionally written to give greater perspective to someone who was not there. This last reason may be why God gives us a different view of his creation of man in Genesis 2. In his second account, God shows us why he did certain things in the creation process and sets the stage for the aftermath.[3]

God begins this second look at his creating activity by giving us a description of the earth before he had completed his refinements. "This is the account about the development of the heavens and the earth when they were created, in the day that the LORD God made the earth and the heavens: No bushes that grow in the field were yet on the earth, and no plants of the field had yet sprung up, since the LORD God had not yet caused it to rain on the earth. There was not yet a man to till the soil, but water came up from the earth and watered the entire surface of the ground" (Genesis 2:4-6). Already while the earth was still relatively barren, God had chosen what would be necessary to support man, even though he had not yet put these things in place. Man was, indeed, God's focal point in his creation. The rest of creation was merely the stage set.

The Bible tells us that God's creation of man was different from his creation of other objects. The other objects, whether animate or inanimate, came into existence, either *ex nihilo* or from previously created materials, at the word of the LORD. Man, however, was created with special attention to detail. "The LORD God formed the man from the dust of the ground and breathed into his nostrils the breath of life, and the man became a living being" (Genesis 2:7). Man was formed from the earth on which he would live, and therefore he would have a special bond to it. In fact, the Hebrew word for man is *"adam,"* which also became his name, and the Hebrew word for ground is *"adamah."* In addition, man also had a direct connection to God who breathed the breath of life into him. The details of the way God did this were not pro-

---

[3] Genesis 2:4-4:26 is often called the "first toledot[h]" in Genesis. A toledot is a Hebrew literary structure that groups events related to a generation or family. Genesis 1:1-2:3 is called the "prologue."

vided to us. Man was thus composed of the ground and of the breath of God, and he was also given the image of God in the process. Moreover, God established a place to put his special creature. "The LORD God planted a garden in Eden in the east, and there he put the man whom he had formed. Out of the ground the LORD God made every kind of tree grow—trees that are pleasant to look at and good for food, including the Tree of Life in the middle of the garden and the Tree of the Knowledge of Good and Evil" (Genesis 2:8,9).

Relative to his description of the rest of his creation, God went into extensive detail about the Garden of Eden. In verse 9 he told us about the two trees that would be of paramount importance in the short-term for the future of mankind. Then God continued with his overview of the layout of the garden. "A river went out from Eden to water the garden, and from there it divided and became the headwaters of four rivers. The name of the first river is Pishon. It flows through the whole land of Havilah, where there is gold, and the gold of that land is good. Incense and onyx stone are also found there. The name of the second river is Gihon. It is the same river that winds through the whole land of Cush. The name of the third river is Tigris. This is the one which flows along the east side of Assyria. The fourth river is the Euphrates" (Genesis 2:10-14). We can see in the detail of the garden, which God inspired Moses to record, the importance of mankind's role in God's plans. God gave this detail because he wanted his chosen people to understand what he had done for them, going way back to when he created the first man. His creation of man had happened in a real place.

God then continued with the commands he had begun in Genesis 1. "The LORD God took the man and settled him in the Garden of Eden to work it and to take care of it. The LORD God gave a command to the man. He said, 'You may freely eat from every tree in the garden, but you shall not eat from the Tree of the Knowledge of Good and Evil, for on the day that you eat from it, you will certainly die'" (Genesis 2:15-17). Man was given the responsibility to care for the garden, a task that must have seemed easy because of the quality of God's workmanship in creating it. Man was also given a warning. It was a reminder that God had a right to place restrictions on mankind that mankind needed to respect as part of his position vis-à-vis his Creator.

In addition to his description of the garden that would be mankind's home, God revealed details about his creation of a wife for Adam. These details were not mentioned in the Genesis 1 account. In Genesis 2 we learn that Adam had been initially created without a wife. God wanted to convince Adam, a ration-

Man – God's Special Creation

al being, by means of a demonstration that there was no suitable companion for him among all the rest of God's kinds. "The LORD God said, 'It is not good for the man to be alone. I will make a helper who is a suitable partner for him.' Out of the soil the LORD God had formed every wild animal and every bird of the sky, and he brought them to the man to see what he would call them. Whatever the man called every living creature, that became its name" (Genesis 2:18,19). To show man the breadth of his creation, God brought the various animal kinds to Adam so he would learn to recognize them and know them by the names that he was permitted to choose for them. There is a clue in these verses that God did not bring all the animals to Adam. For example, no mention is made of fish. Yet, it appears all the kinds of the land animals and those of the sky were brought to Adam. This certainly implies the number of kinds could not have been too extensive because Adam accomplished the task of naming before the creation of woman. We know from Genesis 1 that this also was completed on the sixth day.

Adam did his job. "The man gave names to all the livestock, and to the birds of the sky, and to every wild animal, but for Adam no helper was found who was a suitable partner for him" (Genesis 2:20). God's demonstration was successful. Adam found no suitable mate, so God acted to give Adam a mate. "The LORD God caused the man to fall into a deep sleep. As the man slept, the LORD God took a rib and closed up the flesh where it had been. The LORD God built a woman from the rib that he had taken from the man and brought her to the man" (Genesis 2:21,22). By using this procedure, God accomplished several important things. First, he made the whole human race out of one initial creature. The woman was of the same quality as the man because they came out of one body, one flesh. Second, God showed he could work outside the laws of nature to change the structure of one living thing into another. A woman is to some extent genetically different from a man; therefore, God had to do genetic engineering in forming her. Finally, God was able to cause such changes instantly. He did not need to allow a long period of time to elapse for them to happen by some natural process.

Having created the woman, God brought her to Adam to be his wife. What joy there must have been when he saw this perfect mate whom God had created for him! "The man said, 'Now this one is bone of my bones and flesh of my flesh. She will be called "woman," because she was taken out of man'" (Genesis 2:23). Hebrew, like many other languages, has a word for "woman" that has the same root as the word for "man." Adam used this word pair to indicate his acceptance that this woman was of the same substance and was in the same image of God that he was. How could they be more alike? While God had given them different roles, nevertheless, having the image of God, they would always be likeminded and live together harmoniously.[4]

The next statement in the Bible has been a puzzle for theologians. It reads, "For this reason a man will leave his father and his mother and will remain united with his wife, and they will become one flesh" (Genesis 2:24). It is natural for us to ask, "Who said it?" If it was said by Adam, he was speaking of things of which he had no knowledge. He had yet to encounter another human being other than the just-introduced woman. He had no experience with fathers, mothers, families, or the concept of leaving one family to found another. While God could have revealed hidden information to him as he sometimes did to the prophets, prophets always spoke in the context of things that they had experienced, not on issues completely unknown. If it was said by God, as might be hinted at by Matthew 19:4 (see footnote 6), then it would be the only statement made by God in the creation account where he was not identified as the speaker. Moreover, the statement is not so much a command as an observation of what was to happen. The reason they would become united was because God had created woman for man. Finally, the statement could be commentary on the situation by Moses, the writer of Genesis, as he similarly did in Genesis 32:32.[5] Moses would have understood the significance of what had occurred.

No matter who made this statement, it is God's revelation concerning the nature of marriage that he established by creating woman from man and for man. After their marriage, a man and a woman, i.e., a husband and his wife, are to be permanently united in intent and in action as if they were still physically one body, just as they were before God separated them. A man should no more divorce his wife, so long as she is faithful, than he should mutilate his body by cutting off his right arm. Marriage, since it was instituted on the sixth day of creation in God's perfect world, was intended to involve complete

---

[4] Some people might fault God for not making everyone with the same characteristics so that all could bear children, either through self-fertilization or binary fission, or through mating with any other human. It is not our place to tell God, who is omniscient and wise, how he should have designed his creation. In regard to this, Isaiah wrote, "Should the creation say to the creator, 'You know nothing'?" (Isaiah 29:16)

[5] For that reason, to this day the people of Israel do not eat the tendon of the hip that is on the socket of the thigh, because God touched the socket of Jacob's thigh on the tendon of the hip. (Genesis 32:32)

Man – God's Special Creation

commitment.[6] This verse, however, should not be overread to claim that there is a union between the souls of a husband and his wife,[7] nor should it be narrowly viewed as referring to a sexual union, which is not a permanent event.

Finally, the Bible talks about "shame." "They were both naked, the man and his wife, and they were not ashamed" (Genesis 2:25). We are ashamed when we cannot stand with integrity before someone. If we know we have done something offensive, or if our clothes are torn, or if our faces are dirty, we feel ashamed to appear before someone who has a right to expect better of us. Because Adam and the woman were perfect, they did not feel ashamed to stand before each other or God without covering. They had nothing evil or imperfect to hide. In Genesis 3, sin would change that.

The Fall into Sin

God did not give us the details concerning how he intended events to play out in the sinless world. He may have given Adam and the yet unnamed woman numerous ideas and commands concerning how to manage the Garden of Eden. If he had, they would have rejoiced in his advice and instruction because they were in his image. We can wonder "What if" about many situations, but this is pointless and dangerous because we cannot know information of this era that has not been revealed. Our speculation was made useless long ago by the tragedy of man's fall into sin.

We need to momentarily digress here to consider the other intelligent beings whom God created. We know almost nothing about his creation of the angels. They clearly existed by the beginning of Genesis 2. Because God created everything in six days, based on his own claim (Exodus 20:11), their creation occurred during that period. We also know some of the angels rebelled and were cast out of God's heavenly presence into eternal suffering.[8] We do not know how many angels were involved or exactly when the rebellion

---

[6] [Jesus said,] "Haven't you read that from the beginning their Maker 'made them male and female,' and said, 'For this reason a man will leave his father and mother and be united to his wife, and the two will be one flesh'? So they are no longer two, but one flesh. Therefore what God has joined together, man must not separate." (Matthew 19:4-6)

[7] Marriage is a temporal union as Jesus indicated in Matthew 22:30. In heaven people will be unmarried as are the angels. The concept of "soul union" has no scriptural basis.

[8] For if God did not spare angels when they sinned but handed them over to chains of darkness by casting them into hell, to be kept under guard for judgment. (2 Peter 2:4)

occurred. It had to have happened after the sixth day because at the end of the sixth day everything was still "very good" (Genesis 1:31). We also do not know the amount of time that passed between the angel's rebellion and the events of Genesis 3 described below.

Satan, here referred to as "the serpent," was the leader of the rebellion against God.[9] The exact form he took here is uncertain, but it was best represented by the Hebrew word for "serpent." Satan started by trying to introduce doubt into the woman's mind. "Now the serpent was more clever than any wild animal which the LORD God had made. He said to the woman, 'Has God really said, "You shall not eat from any tree in the garden" ?'" (Genesis 3:1). Any perfect intelligent being created by God would have known the answer to that question or would not have cared. That anything would ask that question should have been a tipoff there was something wrong.

The woman, however, foolishly took up the conversation. In a world where there were few chances for conversation, perhaps this is not surprising. The woman answered the serpent, "We may eat fruit from the trees of the garden, but not from the fruit of the tree that is in the middle of the garden. God has said, 'You shall not eat from it. You shall not touch it, or else you will die'" (Genesis 3:2,3). In her enthusiasm to respond, she may have embroidered on the command of God, not only in words but in concept, by adding the word "touch." Was she intentionally making the commandment of God seem more onerous than it was? Had she started leaning toward Satan's thinking? Satan sensed she was wavering, so he continued. "The serpent said to the woman, 'You certainly will not die. In fact, God knows that the day you eat from it, your eyes will be opened, and you will be like God, knowing good and evil'" (Genesis 3:4,5). Satan judged it was time for a strategic lie. He directly contradicted God, giving the woman a clear choice of actions—obey God and ignore Satan or bet that Satan was telling her what God did not want her to know. The whole of God's perfect physical creation hung in the balance, and she yielded. Her husband stood there and apparently said nothing. "When the woman saw that the tree was good for food, and that it was appealing to the eyes, and that the tree was desirable to make one wise, she took some of its fruit and ate. She also gave some to her husband, who was with her, and he ate it. The eyes of both of them were opened, and they realized that they were

---

[9] The great dragon was thrown down—the ancient serpent, the one called the Devil and Satan, the one who leads the whole inhabited earth astray—he was thrown down to the earth, and his angels were thrown down with him. (Revelation 12:9)

Man – God's Special Creation

naked. They sewed fig leaves together and made coverings for their waists. They heard the voice of the LORD God, who was walking around in the garden during the cooler part of the day, and the man and his wife hid themselves from the presence of the LORD God among the trees of the garden" (Genesis 3:6-8).

In Psalm 1, God would warn people against the lure of progressive evil. The psalmist wrote, "How blessed is the man who does not walk in the advice of the wicked, who does not stand on the path with sinners, and who does not sit in a meeting with mockers. But his delight is in the teaching of the LORD" (Psalm 1:1,2a). "Walk," "stand," and "sit" are used to indicate progressive activities that get a person more deeply involved in evil rather than in the LORD's teaching. In the same way, Eve first saw "good for food," then "appealing," and finally "desirable to make one wise." At that point she had given her heart to her selfish desires, and all was lost.

With Adam's and his wife's eating and hiding in shame, the creation account was over because God's perfect creation had been contaminated by sin. Adam and his wife immediately knew this. Something had changed, and they wanted to hide, from each other (at least partially) and from God. Satan knew it, and he waited and watched with anticipation to see what God would do because he had succeeded in ruining what God had so carefully created. Finally, God knew it the instant it happened because he is omniscient. How would God respond? God's response was as overarching as had been his creation. It is the subject of chapter 8.

Old Testament History

After man had sinned, God could have immediately destroyed all evidence that man had ever existed and started over. That would have been our way. When we make something and it doesn't turn out as we hoped, we are often quick to discard it and begin again. We hope to do better the second time, using what we learned from the errors we made in our first attempt. God, however, knew how to do things right the first time, so our human practices are not relevant to him. Conversely, because God is just and hates sin, he could have sentenced man to eternal punishment immediately, just as he did Satan and the demons. He did neither. Even apart from his plan of salvation, which will be discussed in chapter 8, God did not completely disown man or treat him like the animals. God continued to acknowledge his creation of man, even when that was distasteful. Let us consider some of the verses in which he spoke about his creation of man and its aftermath.

Moses wrote about how the situation regarding man grieved God, as when a person has done something that turned out badly. "The LORD regretted that he had made man on the earth, and his heart was filled with sorrow" (Genesis 6:6). This verse uses a personification of God as though he considered the thorough corruption of his special creature in the same way that a parent might consider a child who has become outrageously bad. Despite this evil situation, God was still willing to protect the lives of people from murder by other people and animals. He commanded, "Whoever sheds man's blood, by man his blood shall be shed, for God made man in his own image" (Genesis 9:6). Moreover, God wanted man to remember who had created him. "So ask now about the former days, long before your time, beginning from the day when God created man on the earth" (Deuteronomy 4:32a).

The Wisdom Literature

Kings David and Solomon recognized God's work in his original creation but also his continuing work in creating each new generation. Despite man's sinful nature, God continued to give man the advantage of a healthy body and a sound mind. David wrote, "I praise you because I am fearfully and wonderfully made. Your works are wonderful, and my soul knows that very well. My bones were not hidden from you when I was made in the secret place, when I was woven together in the depths of the earth. Your eyes saw my unfinished body. In your book all of them were written. Days were determined, before any of them existed" (Psalm 139:14-16).

Solomon more philosophically looked at man and his existence upon the earth. He wrote, "Rich and poor have this in common: The LORD is the maker of them all" (Proverbs 22:2). All people are connected by being descended from God's original creation of man. Later, Solomon acknowledged the situation that he found in his consideration of the nature of man. He wrote, "Look, I have found only this: I have found that God made mankind upright, but they have gone off looking for many schemes" (Ecclesiastes 7:29). Finally, he noted that we must prepare for the end of our lives, no matter whether we have been great or small in our own eyes or in the eyes of others. "Remember your Creator before…the dust [the body of man] goes back into the ground—just as it was before, and the spirit goes back to God who gave it" (Ecclesiastes 12:6,7).

The Prophets

While numerous Old Testament prophets alluded to the power of God and to the need for man to acknowledge God's almighty hand in all matters of human life, it was Isaiah who continually reminded the people that everything, including their very selves, belonged to God and that they were to obey his commands. This was not a new condition, as it went back to the creation of man. Isaiah wrote, "This is what the LORD, your Maker, says, the LORD who formed you from the womb, who will help you" (Isaiah 44:2a). In this passage he stressed God's creation of the individual. Later he pointed out that our creation was more than just our personal selves. Our creator is also the Creator of everything. "You have forgotten the LORD, your Creator, who stretches out the heavens, who makes the earth stand firm" (Isaiah 51:13). Finally, Isaiah spoke of the personal interest that God takes in his children. We are more than just "things"; we are part of God's family that he does not wish to abandon. Nevertheless, this personal God is still omnipotent. "[B]ecause your Maker is your husband.[10] The LORD of Armies is his name" (Isaiah 54:5a).

The New Testament

Both Jesus and the apostles in the New Testament pointed people to the creation of man at the very beginning of the world. For example, Jesus related marriage in his era to the first marriage of Adam and Eve and reminded people that the unchanging God demanded the same rules applied in all periods of history. He said, "But from the beginning of creation, God made them male and female. For this reason a man will leave his father and mother and be joined to his wife, and the two will become one flesh. So they are no longer two but one flesh. Therefore, what God has joined together, let no one separate" (Mark 10:6-9). To God, marriage was marriage. It was his institution, and he did not intend for it to be disrupted by changing human opinions.

As the apostles went forth to preach the Gospel, they encountered people of many nationalities. While the Jews had always regarded themselves as a

---

[10] In the Old Testament a husband was expected to provide for all the needs of his wife.

special people due to their relationship with Abraham, this racial pride could not be permitted in the Christian church. God sent his missionaries to preach to everyone because everyone needed his message. St. Paul said to the Athenians, "From one man, he [the LORD] made every nation of mankind to live over the entire face of the earth" (Acts 17:26). In his epistle to the Corinthians, St. Paul emphasized that there had been an order in God's creation and that the order was important to the lives of God's children. He wrote, "For man is not from woman, but woman from man, and man was not created for the woman, but woman for the man" (1 Corinthians 11:8-10). Man and woman both had a role in God's plan for the world and the church, and those roles were not the same.

St. Peter also called on people to acknowledge their Creator, especially when things were difficult. He wrote, "So let those who suffer according to the will of God entrust their souls to their faithful Creator while doing what is good" (1 Peter 4:19).

The creation of man was the highpoint of God's physical creative activity. He revealed his formation of man to a far greater extent than any other part of his creation. In fact, many parts of God's creation, e.g., angels and microorganisms, are not described in the Scriptures. Even when man went astray, God did not disown him, although God did destroy the great majority of the people through the flood. God has sustained his creation, both inanimate and living, since the first day of its existence. We will next turn to God's preservation as a necessary extension of his creating work.

7

Preservation – God's Continuing Work of Creation

We generally think of creation as something that God did in the first six days of the world's existence. Because Genesis 2:1 says, "The heavens and the earth were finished, along with everything in them," we are tempted to believe God never created anything after the sixth day. That would be overreading the Scriptures and tying God's hands. A psalmist wrote, "In fact, our God is in the heavens. He does everything that pleases him" (Psalm 115:3). In reading the Bible, we must always be careful not to restrict God more than he has restricted himself. He cannot be bound by logic, by reason, or by precedent, only by his own specific words. In this chapter we will look at how God extensively used his creative power throughout history.

God's "Creative Hands"

God can create in two ways. First, he can make something out of nothing (*ex nihilo*) as we saw in chapter 3. This is how he created the world on the first day and how he created many things on days two through six as well. God did not relinquish that ability when he finished "the heavens and the earth." He can create more material in the universe any time he deems it desirable, as when Jesus fed thousands of people from meager food supplies (Matthew 14:13-21 and 15:32-38). Regarding this, however, we must be careful because we have no promise from God that he will perform similar creative events in the future. Second, God can "create" by using materials that already exist and reshaping them in some manner so they will serve a completely different purpose. For example, God "formed the man from the dust of the ground" (Genesis 2:7). As the eternal intelligent being, God took what existed and, in his wisdom, transformed the dust into something else. This is the same usage of the word "create" we employ when we say that a person has "created" something. A person does not bring matter into existence from nothing but uses what is available. The only difference between God and humankind in this usage of the word is that God can transform matter in ways that far exceed anything that we can do or imagine.

In the Bible God uses his almighty power in two ways to preserve his creation and to accomplish his divine will.[1] To aid us in understanding these ways, we might personify God's behavior by saying he has two creative "hands."[2] The first hand we might call his "natural" hand. Much of his preservation of his creation is done through the "laws of nature." These are the regular patterns of behavior that God uses to direct the various objects, objects that he created from nothing, to follow until he gives them different commands. Scientists can learn about these laws of nature by studying the physical universe. By using his natural hand in a predictable way, God allows people to give an explanation to what they observe and to make plans for their futures. God gave us assurance that he would manage things in this manner when he said, "While the earth remains, seedtime and harvest, cold and heat, summer and winter, and day and night shall not cease" (Genesis 8:22). Yet, even when using his natural hand, God is quite able to "tweak" the components of nature to cause the outcome of natural processes to be what he desires. Solomon wrote, "Lots are cast into the pouch, but the LORD determines all their decisions" (Proverbs 16:33). God can effectively "fly under the radar" of human observations because natural processes have statistical variation, causing individual components of a system to behave somewhat differently from each other. God's divinely effective actions can be hidden within normal statistical deviation of natural processes.

God can, of course, act directly upon nature with his "supernatural" hand. This happens when God performs an overt miracle that exceeds what could happen by natural processes. For example, God caused the waters of the Jordan to "pile up" at the town of Adam and not flow down the Jordan valley until the Israelites had crossed the riverbed on dry ground (Joshua 3:14-17). God

---

[1] The concept of God using his almighty power in two ways is from our perspective, not from God's. God does not differentiate between what we regard as "natural acts" and what we regard as "supernatural acts." God always directs and sustains all things in the same manner to conform to his will regardless of how it appears to us.

[2] Eggert, "Creation vs. Science."

Preservation

can perform such actions anytime he desires, and it does not require a human observer to validate that God has done such a miracle. We noted in chapter 4 that many things God created in the first six days to support what he told us he created were not specifically mentioned. However, what was mentioned documents he had made these unmentioned things as well. God acts by natural and supernatural methods as he chooses and when he chooses because to him, they are really the same.

The Old Testament

We might imagine that God's preservation of the natural world would be accomplished merely by keeping things humming along smoothly using the laws of nature that he created. Yet, in a sin-tainted world, everything was not going to run smoothly. The first problem was man, that creature corrupted by sin. Mankind was going to disrupt the events of nature, intentionally or not, by his self-centeredness. Second, once sin had entered the world, animals, such as beavers and beetles, were going to destroy trees which might cause secondary effects, such as landslides or floods. Lightning was going to start wildfires. Through the scientific study of many areas of nature, we now know almost all natural processes are controlled by complex non-linear differential equations and will degenerate into some form of chaotic behavior as time passes.[3] For God's will to be done, therefore, he needs to engage in active management of all natural systems.

As we look at the creative acts that God uses to preserve his world, it sometimes initially appears he has been destroying his universe rather than maintaining it. This, however, is because our view is not God's view. God can always see the big picture, and he knows whether changes that seem destructive or harmful to us are indeed the right actions to take to accomplish his ultimate goal, which is the salvation of his elect.

After mankind sinned, God could not let people continue to enjoy his blessing of a perfect world. That would have caused them to become bolder and bolder in defying him. He therefore cursed the ground so it would no longer produce necessary food for human survival without a struggle. God said, "Thorns and thistles will spring up from the ground for you" (Genesis

---

[3] Steven Strogatz, *Chaos*, The Great Courses (Chantilly, Virginia: The Teaching Company, 2008).

3:18a). New or altered types of plants, which were not the fruitful plants from the initial creation, would begin to spread over the soil that Adam needed to cultivate.

Mankind has always been a slow learner. Despite the hardships God laid upon people, people became even worse in their rebellious behavior. When God had enough of human insolence, he determined to intervene to bring about a catastrophic flood that would destroy most of the human and animal life on the planet. God said, "I myself am about to bring a flood of waters on the earth, in order to destroy all flesh under the sky that has the breath of life" (Genesis 6:17a). He intervened to manipulate the forces of nature to accomplish his goals and then to clean up the planet afterward to make it again habitable. One thing he created in the process was the desire in just the right animals to come to Noah to be loaded into the ark. Noah did not have to travel the whole surface of the earth to find them based on a list that God had handed him. God brought together the animals so Noah could carry out his command. We read, "Clean animals, animals that are not clean, birds, and everything that creeps on the ground went into the ark with Noah two by two (male and female), just as God had commanded Noah" (Genesis 7:8,9). After the flood had accomplished its purpose and God had again set Noah on firm ground, he created a new sign in the heavens to assure mankind of his commitment to them. He said to Noah, "I have set my rainbow in the cloud, and it will be the sign of a covenant between me and the earth" (Genesis 9:13). We do not know how God altered the planet Earth or its interaction with light to create the rainbow or give it a special prominence, but we take God at his word that he did what was necessary to produce it. He who created the sun without explaining it to us could certainly likewise create the rainbow.

God also changed man's diet after the flood, saying, "Every living, moving thing will be food for you. I have given everything to you, just as I gave you the green plants" (Genesis 9:3). Whether it was at this time or earlier that God allowed animals to eat other animals is unknown. Since the digestive tracts of herbivores and carnivores are significantly different, however, God's creative hand had to be involved in some manner to make the appropriate alterations in carnivores' DNA to produce such biological changes.

We should at this point recognize that just as God did not reveal to us everything that he did during the first six days of creation, so he was under no obligation to reveal to us any earth-shaping actions he took during the flood. This has historically been a fertile field for fruitless speculation. We cannot

Preservation

know what God does not reveal to us. We do not know what the world looked like before the flood, so we have no starting point to postulate what God did to get us to the world that we are able to observe today. We do not know how much he worked with his "natural" hand and how much he worked with his "supernatural" hand in re-creating the post-flood world. We do not know, and we cannot know, as will be discussed in greater detail in chapter 13. We are informationally blind in this matter, and as Jesus said, "[I]f the blind are guiding the blind, both will fall into a pit" (Matthew 15:14b).

The LORD wanted the whole earth populated, as he commanded in Genesis 9:1.[4] When the people failed to follow God's command, he created an inability for people to understand each other so they could not readily work together, thereby causing them to separate and populate the whole earth. "So the LORD scattered them from there over the face of the whole earth, and they stopped building the city. It was named Babel, because there the LORD confused the language of the whole earth. From there the LORD scattered them over the face of the whole earth" (Genesis 11:8,9). Later, when God needed to preserve his chosen people from those who were excessively evil, he created a destructive rain of sulfur and fire. "Then the LORD rained on Sodom and Gomorrah sulfur and fire out of the sky from the LORD. He overthrew those cities, as well as all the plain, all the inhabitants of the cities, and whatever grew in the soil" (Genesis 19:24,25). In each of these circumstances, the LORD used his creative powers to change the world situation in such a manner as to carry out his will. God can even transform evil intent into good for his people, as when Joseph was sold into slavery by his brothers but became the ruler of Egypt (Genesis 50:19-21).

Several times during the exodus of the Israelites from Egypt, the LORD promised he would intervene in nature to bless them and create favorable conditions for them if they remained faithful to his covenant. They did not need to fear what other people had to fear in this sinful world because the LORD was their strong deliverer. Moses conveyed this promise to the people, "He will love you and bless you and multiply you. He will bless the fruit from your womb and the fruit from your soil, your grain and your new wine and your fresh olive oil, the offspring of your cattle and the young of your flock

---

[4] God blessed Noah and his sons and said to them, "Be fruitful and multiply and fill the earth." (Genesis 9:1)

upon the land that he swore to your fathers that he would give you. You will be blessed beyond all the peoples. There will not be an infertile male or infertile female among you or among your livestock. The LORD will remove from you all sickness, and he will not place on you all of the diseases of Egypt, the calamities that you experienced. Instead he will put them on all those who hate you" (Deuteronomy 7:13-15). On the other hand, the LORD promised to use his power over the earth against them if they disobeyed his covenant. Moses wrote, "The LORD will send on you a curse and confusion and opposition in every undertaking of your hand that you carry out, until you are destroyed and until you quickly perish, because of the evil you have done by forsaking me. The LORD will cause epidemics to cling to you until he has removed you from your land that you are going to possess. The LORD will strike you with wasting diseases, fever, and inflammation, with intense heat and with drought, and with blight and with mildew. They will pursue you until you perish. The skies over your head will become bronze, and the earth under you will become iron. The LORD will turn the rain of your land to dust. From the heavens it will come down on you until you are destroyed" (Deuteronomy 28:20-24). The LORD wanted to preserve his people, but if they deserted him, he was committed to arraying nature against them. They would know in one way or the other that he was omnipotent because nature would obey him and him alone.

The Old Testament abounds with accounts of God using his creative powers to intervene to save his people from the physical dangers posed by their enemies, from a lack of food, and from their own arrogance. Let us remind ourselves of some of these incidents. When God's people were fleeing Pharaoh's army, a strong east wind opened a way through the Red Sea for them (Exodus 14:21). When the Israelites lacked food in the wilderness, God sent manna for forty years (Exodus 16:14,15). When faced with the walled city of Jericho, the LORD caused the walls to fall flat so the city could be easily captured (Joshua 6:20). God stopped the sun and the moon from moving across the sky for a whole day (Joshua 10:13,14). God gave Samson superhuman powers (Judges 13-16). The LORD sent a plague that killed 70,000 people to punish David for taking a census of the people of Israel (2 Samuel 24:15,16a). God twice sent fire at Elijah's request to kill those ordered to take him prisoner (2 Kings 1:9-12). When Elisha prayed to God, he created life again in the son of the Shunamite woman (2 Kings 4:32-35). God blinded an entire army at the request of Elisha (2 Kings 6:17-20). God sent an angel to kill 185,000 Assyrian soldiers to save Hezekiah and Jerusalem (2 Kings 19:35,36). Many more examples could be cited to show how God used his power over nature to accomplish his purposes by creating sequences of events that could not have occurred through the laws of nature. The LORD can create and re-create the things of the physical universe at his pleasure.

The Wisdom Literature

In the biblical wisdom literature, we see how God's people recognized the hand of the LORD working even within the common activities that seemed to occur naturally. We also see God personally reminding his people of his concern for them and of his active control of their circumstances. Let us begin with Job.

In trying to help Job understand his miserable situation, Eliphaz the Temanite said, "He [God] does great things that are beyond investigation, and miracles that are too many to be counted. He provides rain for the earth. He waters the fields in the countryside" (Job 5:9,10). Eliphaz recognized God actively preserves the earth. Later Job said, "You [God] clothed me with skin and flesh. You wove me together with bones and tendons. You provided me with life and mercy, and your watchful care has guarded my spirit" (Job 10:11,12). Job affirmed that our very lives come into existence as an act of God. Finally, when Job felt God had wronged him, God personally reminded Job that it was the LORD who controls all things and who provides for everything. In this discourse the LORD said to Job, "Who prepares its provisions for the raven, when its young are screaming to God, while they thrash around in the nest waiting for food?" (Job 38:41).

King David was a man after his [the LORD's] own heart (1 Samuel 13:14) and the pleasant singer of Israel's songs (2 Samuel 23:1). In the psalms David wrote about how the LORD cared for him personally but also cared for all his people and, indeed, for all the creatures upon earth. Let us start by considering Psalm 23 in which David declared God to be a shepherd, the profession at which he himself had worked early in his life. Just as shepherds needed to be very diligent in caring for their sheep, so the LORD has been very diligent in caring for us. In another psalm David noted the LORD gives special care to his elect. "Love the LORD, all his favored ones! The LORD preserves the faithful, but he pays back in full the one who acts proudly" (Psalm 31:23). Things went from bad to worse for David when members of his own tribe tried to betray him to Saul; still David wrote, "Indeed, God is my helper. The LORD is the one who preserves my life" (Psalm 54:4). David trusted the LORD to create a way for him to escape any trap. When in danger David prayed to God who had the power to act against any enemy that David might face. He wrote, "For the sake of your name, O LORD, preserve my life. In your righteousness, bring me out of trouble. In your mercy, wipe out my enemies, and destroy all who threaten my life, for I am your servant" (Psalm 143:11,12).

David, however, did not just write about how he knew the LORD would bless and rescue him but also about how God would use his creative power to provide for all men and beasts. He wrote, "You visit the earth and water it. You make it very rich. God's stream is filled with water. You provide grain for them, just as you planned. You drench the land's furrows. You flatten its plowed ground. You soften it with showers. You bless its crops. You crown the year with your goodness. The tracks made by your carts overflow with riches. The pastures of the wilderness drip. The hills are wrapped with joy. The meadows are clothed with flocks. The valleys are dressed with grain. They shout for joy. Yes! They sing" (Psalm 65:9-13) and "The eyes of all look eagerly to you, and you give them their food at the proper time. He opens his hand, and he satisfies the desire of every living thing" (Psalm 145:15,16).

David was not the only psalmist to recognize the direct intervention of the LORD in nature. Another wrote, "He is the one who has preserved our lives. He did not let our feet slip" (Psalm 66:9). Still another psalmist noted how dependent all life forms were upon God when he wrote, "All of them [the animals] wait hopefully for you to give them their food in its time. You give it to them. They gather it up. You open your hand. They are satisfied with good things. You hide your face. They are terrified. You take away their breath. They breathe their last and return to their dust. You send your Spirit—they are created. You renew the face of the earth" (Psalm 104:27-30).

King Solomon also recognized the involvement of the LORD in the things of nature. God's hands were behind whatever happened, but particularly they were present to protect his children and preserve them from the wicked. Solomon wrote, "He [the LORD] protects those who walk on paths of justice. He guards the way of his favored ones" (Proverbs 2:8). Solomon observed that the LORD intervenes to help the needy. "The LORD will not allow the righteous to starve" (Proverbs 10:3a). In fact, the LORD may bless a person with wealth and happiness. "The blessing of the LORD makes a person wealthy, and he adds no sorrow to it" (Proverbs 10:22). The LORD can even do what seems contrary to the natural order of things. "The LORD tears down the house of the arrogant, but he maintains the property line of a widow" (Proverbs 15:25). Throughout Proverbs Solomon stressed the wisdom of following the LORD and being blessed rather than becoming enmeshed in folly and receiving the LORD's curse. Finally, as an observer of the long-term futility of human effort, Solomon wrote that God could give short-term satisfaction, "Likewise, for everyone to whom God has given wealth and riches, if God has also given him ability to eat from it, to enjoy his reward, and to rejoice in the results of his hard work—this is a gift of God" (Ecclesiastes 5:19).

The Prophets

The prophets in the Old Testament were sent to warn the descendants of Jacob that if they abandoned the LORD, he would abandon them. While sometimes they did speak of God's physical providence, more frequently their message was centered on how God had brought his people to their present era. Nonetheless, the people were warned they should not use this history to assume God would protect them in the future if they continued to disobey him. Considering some passages in Isaiah will give us a good sense of how the prophets spoke about the way the LORD would use his power for the benefit of his people and his honor.

Isaiah began with the LORD's lament. "Hear this, O heavens, and listen, O earth, for the LORD has spoken. I have raised children and brought them up, but they have rebelled against me" (Isaiah 1:2). In these verses the LORD stated he had used his power to establish the Israelites, but they had turned their backs on him. Despite this, God promised that, at least for the immediate future, he would protect his holy city. "Like a hovering bird, the LORD of Armies will protect Jerusalem. He will protect it and deliver it" (Isaiah 31:5a). As time passed, however, the LORD felt he needed to point out that even the dumb animals held him in higher regard than his own people. "The wild animals, the jackals and ostriches, will honor me, because I am providing water in the wilderness, rivers in a parched wasteland, water for my chosen people to drink" (Isaiah 43:20). God continued to provide for the children of Israel, but they acted as if they were on their own and as if their God were helpless to deal with their real problems. The LORD finally asked, "Is my arm really too short to redeem? Do I not have enough power to rescue? Yes! By my rebuke I can dry up the sea. I can turn rivers into a wilderness, so that their fish will stink from having no water, and they will die of thirst" (Isaiah 50:2b). God even promised to help a heathen king rescue his people. The LORD said to Cyrus, "I myself will go before you, and I will level high mountains. I will break bronze doors into pieces, and I will cut through iron bars" (Isaiah 45:2).

Jeremiah had to preach doom and despair because there was no longer the possibility Judah would be spared. Nevertheless, he personally did not forget the power of the LORD when he wrote, "Do the worthless idols of the nations send rain? Do the skies provide the torrential showers? Is it not rather you, who are the LORD our God? Our hope is in you, because you are the one who does all these things" (Jeremiah 14:22).

The text of the book of Jonah shows the detailed involvement of the LORD in the lives of his people. God created a storm to end Jonah's journey to Tarshish, but then he ended the storm and rescued Jonah when the time was right. "Then the LORD provided a large fish to swallow Jonah, and Jonah was in the belly of the fish three days and three nights" (Jonah 1:17). When Jonah was unhappy about having succeeded in bringing the people of Nineveh to repentance, the LORD intervened directly several times to bring him to his senses. "Then the LORD God provided a plant and made it grow up over Jonah to provide shade over his head, to relieve him from his discomfort. So Jonah was very happy about the plant. But at dawn the next day God provided a worm, and it attacked the plant so that it withered. When the sun rose, God provided a scorching east wind" (Jonah 4:6-8a). We see how emphatic the Scriptures are in asserting all that happened was God's work.

Later, the LORD devastated the land of Judah and sent its people into exile. When he brought the people back, the LORD proclaimed he would once more make the land fertile. He said, "Sowing will take place in peace. The vine will yield its fruit. The earth will yield its produce. The sky will provide its dew" (Zechariah 8:12). Zechariah therefore told the people to seek the help of the LORD for blessings in their agriculture. "Ask the LORD, who makes storm clouds, to give rain at the right time for the spring rains, and he will provide showers of rain, and there will be crops in the field for everyone" (Zechariah 10:1).

The Gospels

In the Gospels we see Jesus both carrying out and discussing God's active intervention in the lives of the people of Israel. God took care of both the people and the animals. Jesus used his creative power to manipulate nature, but he also spoke of how God was caring for his creation even when he was not doing things that attracted people's attention. We will start by reflecting on Jesus' own ministry of active intervention.

Many of Jesus' healing miracles are described in the Gospels, and it is unnecessary to look at each of them to understand he was using his divine power to create new and better circumstances for those around him. Let us consider only a few examples of his work. St. Matthew noted, "Jesus traveled throughout Galilee, teaching in their synagogues, preaching the gospel of the kingdom, and healing every disease and every sickness among the people" (Matthew 4:23). Physical ailments fled at the word of the Creator of all. Jesus could even reverse death itself. "He said, 'Young man, I say to you, get up!' The dead man sat up and began to speak, and Jesus gave him to his mother" (Luke 7:14,15). When John the Baptizer sent his disciples to ask if he was the real Messiah who was to come, Jesus pointed to his power over nature. "Jesus answered them, 'Go, report to John what you hear and see: The blind receive sight, the lame walk, those who have leprosy are cured, the deaf hear, the dead are raised, and the gospel is preached to the poor. Blessed is the one who does not take offense at me'" (Matthew 11:4-6). He also showed he could delegate this healing power to others. He once told his disciples, "As you go, preach this message: 'The kingdom of heaven is near!' Heal the sick. Raise the dead. Cleanse lepers. Drive out demons" (Matthew 10:7,8a). God's supernatural hand was visibly at work while Jesus walked the Earth.

Jesus also directed the people to look around themselves to see how the LORD was working for their good more powerfully than they could imagine. His message of "don't be fearful, trust God" was clear in the words he used during his Sermon on the Mount. Jesus said, "For this reason I tell you, do not worry about your life, what you will eat or drink, or about your body, what you will wear. Is not life more than food and the body more than clothing? Look at the birds of the air. They do not sow or reap or gather into barns, and yet your heavenly Father feeds them. Are you not worth much more than they? Which of you can add a single moment to his lifespan by worrying?

Why do you worry about clothing? Consider how the lilies of the field grow. They do not labor or spin, but I tell you that not even Solomon in all his glory was dressed like one of these. If that is how God clothes the grass of the field, which is alive today and tomorrow is thrown into the furnace, will he not clothe you even more, you of little faith? So do not worry, saying, 'What will we eat?' or 'What will we drink?' or 'What will we wear?' For the unbelievers chase after all these things. Certainly your heavenly Father knows that you need all these things" (Matthew 6:25-32). The great Creator controls nature even when that control is nothing out of the ordinary.

Jesus encouraged the people to call on their heavenly Father for help with complete trust that he would intervene by whatever means was necessary to aid them. He said, "[Y]our Father knows what you need before you ask him. Therefore pray like this: 'Our Father in heaven, hallowed be your name. Your kingdom come. Your will be done on earth as it is in heaven. Give us today our daily bread. Forgive us our debts, as we also forgive our debtors. Lead us not into temptation, but deliver us from evil.'" (Matthew 6:8-13). Physical and particularly spiritual blessings were available to them in abundance for the asking. Jesus assured them God would certainly answer their prayers. "Then if you know how to give good gifts to your children, even though you are evil, how much more will your Father in heaven give good gifts to those who ask him!" (Matthew 7:11). Yet, some people might have thought they were too insignificant for God to waste his power to alter the universe just for them. Jesus answered that worry also. "Are not two sparrows sold for a small coin? Yet not one of them will fall to the ground without the knowledge and consent of your Father. And even the hairs of your head are all numbered. So do not be afraid. You are worth more than many sparrows" (Matthew 10:29-31). As we will see in the next chapter, God's people are worth considerably more than any number of God's other creatures.

The Apostles

When Jesus was about to return to heaven, he commissioned his apostles to carry out his work, and he gave them, in the appropriate measure, the same authority over nature he himself had. They performed miracles using the supernatural hand of God while assuring the people that God could take care of them with his natural hand as well. Let us briefly survey the apostles carrying out their mission.

When told of the death of a valuable Christian in another city, St. Peter traveled there and asked to be alone with the body. "Then he turned toward the body and said, 'Tabitha, get up!' She opened her eyes, and when she saw Peter, she sat up. He gave her his hand and helped her stand up. After he called the saints and the widows, he presented her to them alive" (Acts 9:40,41). Death was no match for the supernatural power of God, even when it was delegated for use by chosen disciples. Nor was it only St. Peter who was delegated this power. "God was doing extraordinary miracles through St. Paul, so that even handkerchiefs or aprons that had touched his skin were carried away to the sick; their illnesses left them and the evil spirits went out of them" (Acts 19:11,12). The LORD could intervene to save even a whole shipload of people, as he promised St. Paul. "[God] said, 'Do not be afraid, Paul. You must stand before Caesar. And surely God has graciously given you all those who are sailing with you.' So keep up your courage, men, because I believe God that it will be exactly the way I have been told" (Acts 27:24,25).

In a world where superstition abounded, St. Paul assured his hearers God's providence was structured with his saints in mind, even if they could not understand it at the time. He wrote to the Romans, "What will we say then? Does this mean that God is unjust? Absolutely not! For God says to Moses: 'I will show mercy to whom I show mercy, and I will have compassion on whom I have compassion.' So then, it does not depend on human desire or effort, but on God's mercy" (Romans 9:14-16). People did not have to worry about whether they had the correct bribe to gain God's favor; all depended on God, not on them. Therefore, they were not to worry. St. Paul wrote to the Philippians, "Do not worry about anything, but in everything, by prayer and petition, with thanksgiving, let your requests be made known to God" (Philippians 4:6).

It was, of course, not only St. Paul who told people about how God's powerful hands were working for them. St. Peter wrote, "Cast all your anxiety on him, because he cares for you" (1 Peter 5:7). St. James, likewise, urged the Christians to rely on the LORD, "Is anyone among you sick? He should call the elders of the church, and they should pray over him, anointing him with oil in the name of the Lord. And the prayer offered in faith will save the sick person, and the Lord will raise him up" (James 5:14,15a). The Scriptures assure us God will respond to prayer, and his answer might be even better than the one we are suggesting to him.

Even this brief survey of God's acts of preservation and rescue shows the power and versatility of the Lord God Almighty. Whether through overt miracles or maneuvering events behind the scenes, his creative power is always at work, even when it is not labeled as such. As the prominent Levite Asaph wrote concerning the LORD, "Call on me in the day of distress. I will deliver you, and you will honor me" (Psalm 50:15) We can depend upon the creative power of God to be employed to preserve his handiwork and to deliver us from every evil of body and soul.

8

God's Re-Creation of Man

There was sheer panic in the air. A man and a woman stood among the trees clothed in aprons made hastily from the leaves of nearby plants. They had never previously made clothes, so the seams probably weren't very smooth. They knew God was coming, and what were they going to do? He had promised them death, and even though they didn't fully comprehend what that meant, it couldn't be good. They would hide, of course, but what good would that do? They knew that God was omniscient, although in their panic maybe they had forgotten that. Anyway, the hour of confrontation was at hand, and Satan was standing by to see just how severely God would treat the victims of his devastatingly evil prank. Enter God.

The Aftermath of Sinning

"The LORD God called to the man and said to him, 'Where are you?'" (Genesis 3:9). This apparently stupid question, since God knew where they were, perhaps brought Adam and his wife back to their senses. Playing hide-and-seek with God was a foolish game. Nevertheless, Adam still did not completely grasp that God knew what they had done. "The man said, 'I heard your voice in the garden, and I was afraid, because I was naked, so I hid myself'" (Genesis 3:10). That Adam was naked had certainly been known by God since the instant he had created Adam, and it had not bothered either God or Adam before. The answer was silly, but Adam was trying to avoid confessing his sin. He fished for another reason that might sound plausible to God, even though fooling God is impossible. Adam should have known better, but we do the same type of thing when we are trying to keep God's eyes off our sinful behavior.

God was not fooled. He continued his line of questioning. "God said, 'Who told you that you were naked? Have you eaten from the tree from which I commanded you not to eat?'" (Genesis 3:11). Since he had not told Adam that he was naked and the concept of nakedness did not exist in man's sinless state, the idea could only have arisen in Adam's mind if he had sinned. God called him on it. Adam again sought to deflect God's accusation. "The man said, 'The woman you gave to be with me—she gave me fruit from the tree, and I ate it'" (Genesis 3:12). Technically, Adam's statement was true. God had given him the woman, and she had given him the fruit from the tree. Nevertheless, Adam's statement was not intended to be a report of the facts but was an effort to shift the blame to his wife and ultimately to God himself. Certainly, the woman and God were more to blame than he was because Adam, at least in his mind, could rationalize that if he had been alone or had not been given a defective wife, he would not have eaten of the tree. Sin had totally changed his attitude toward God and the wife whom God had given him since he spoke in Genesis 2:23.

The woman watched Adam try to get off the hook by shifting the blame to her. Fearing she might be held as solely responsible for the sin, she followed Adam's lead and tried to shift the blame to the only other actor available. "The LORD God said to the woman, 'What have you done?' The woman said, 'The serpent deceived me, and I ate'" (Genesis 3:13). God justly accused her, and she pointed her finger at the serpent. Once again, there was the implication that if God had not acted foolishly in making the serpent, this sin would never have happened. The situation was clear to all. The humans were as guilty as sin of sin, and the judgment of God was about to be issued. For the briefest moment it appeared Satan had won.

The LORD's Unexpected Mercy

One can only imagine the range of punishments that God had available. Adam and the woman certainly sensed they were going to be slapped down hard. A perfect and just God could not tolerate sin, so a new trial period with a second chance seemed out of the question. No, without a doubt, punishment was going to come, and the punishment was going to be severe. And it was severe, only not in the way that anyone of those standing before God could have envisioned.

As was common in Hebrew society, God reversed his order of addressing the issues involved. Satan, who had felt he had won a major victory, quickly

God's Re-Creation of Man

got handed a crushing defeat. "The LORD God said to the serpent, 'Because you have done this, you are cursed more than all the livestock, and more than every wild animal. You shall crawl on your belly, and you shall eat dust all the days of your life. I will put hostility between you and the woman, and between your seed and her seed. He will crush your head, and you will crush his heel'" (Genesis 3:14,15). As noted in chapter 6, "serpent" was the best Hebrew word for the form that Satan took, but we do not really know exactly how Satan appeared when he tempted the woman. In Revelation, Satan is referred to as a "dragon" (Revelation 12:7-9). We also do not know whether Satan occupied a real animal or only came in the form of an animal. It is unimportant. God cursed the animal form Satan took because agents of Satan will share his punishment. Perhaps the "serpent" previously had legs or had the ability to live strictly in trees. We do not know. God used his creative power to reduce this beast to a dirty life on the ground. Satan himself, however, was told he would be crushed, i.e., his power to harm God's elect would be destroyed. This verse therefore gave hope of a Savior for mankind. God promised and God would fulfill. It would not happen right away, but the fulfillment was before the eyes of God when he made the promise. To the timeless God the promise and the fulfillment were simultaneous acts.

We need to pause a moment to consider the word "seed." We commonly think of children as "seeds" of the parents because they grow into the next generation. In fact, sometimes all the descendants of a person are thought of as his or her "seed." In this case, we know the ultimate seed of the woman was Christ.[1] Satan, of course, does not sire or bear natural children because the number of angels and demons are fixed.[2] Satan's "seed" are his followers, both the angels that fell and those people who choose to live in Satan's lies.

God's promised punishment of Satan did not leave the two human beings off the hook. They, too, had been totally corrupted by sin and could not stand before God in all his holiness. God had promised them death if they sinned,[3]

---

[1] The promises God spoke referred to Abraham and to his seed. It doesn't say, "And to seeds," as if it were referring to many, but, as referring to one, "And to your seed," who is Christ. (Galatians 3:16)

[2] [Jesus said,] "In the resurrection people neither marry nor are given in marriage. Instead they are like the angels of God in heaven." (Matthew 22:30) The angels therefore cannot reproduce and are limited in number to those created in the first six days.

[3] [God said,] "But you shall not eat from the Tree of the Knowledge of Good and Evil, for on the day that you eat from it, you will certainly die." (Genesis 2:17)

and death was what they were going to get. However, there would be different types of death. While the promise of Genesis 3:15 could rescue them from eternal death, God would impose on them a burdened life and physical death that would end their physical life. "To the woman he said, 'I will greatly increase your pain in childbearing. With painful labor you will give birth to children. Your desire will be for your husband, but he will rule over you'" (Genesis 3:16). The first creation of people was pleasant for them, even with major surgery on Adam, but when God would create more people within women, it would not be nearly so pleasant. Discomfort and illness in pregnancy and hard labor and pain in childbirth would be common. Moreover, women would have to deal with husbands corrupted by sin who would not always be kind and loving partners. One cannot be the agent of sin without suffering the consequences.

The punishment placed upon Adam reflected his lack of leadership when his wife was tempted. "To Adam he [God] said, 'Because you listened to your wife's voice and ate from the tree about which I commanded you, "You shall not eat from it," the soil is cursed on account of you. You will eat from it with painful labor all the days of your life. Thorns and thistles will spring up from the ground for you, but you will eat the crops of the field. By the sweat of your face you will eat bread until you return to the soil, for out of it you were taken. For you are dust, and to dust you shall return'" (Genesis 3:17-19). As we examine Adam's punishment, we become aware he received several sentences from God. First, God held Adam accountable for his sinning as well as his wife's sinning, even though his wife ate the fruit first.[4] Adam had been created first, and he was the leader. He had failed in that role, so God held him responsible. Second, Adam was cursed with a hard life of laboring against the soil from which he had been taken. The soil was no longer his willing partner, but it had been transformed as discussed in chapter 7. Finally, his body was sentenced to suffer physical death and to return to the soil as if he had never been taken from it. Physically, he had no permanency on earth. Death would always hang over Adam and his descendants.

Before God's curses on mankind were implemented, two symbolic actions occurred. "The man named his wife Eve because she would be the mother of

---

[4] So then, just as sin entered the world through one man and death through sin, so also death spread to all people because all sinned. For even before the law was given, sin was in the world. Now, sin is not charged to one's account if there is no law, and yet death reigned from the time of Adam to the time of Moses, even over those whose sin was not like the transgression of Adam, who is a pattern of the one who was to come. (Romans 5:12-14)

God's Re-Creation of Man

all the living. The LORD God made clothing of animal skins for Adam and for his wife and clothed them" (Genesis 3:20,21). First, Adam finally named his wife, accepting that she had a distinct identity apart from him. In an imperfect world there could no longer be a perfect union between man and woman. Second, God changed the relationship between man and the animals. The lives of animals could henceforth be sacrificed for the benefit of mankind where previously only the plants could be sacrificed for that purpose.

This account closed with Adam and Eve learning the meaning of death—death was separation. God separated them from the source of perpetual life he had given them. "The LORD God said, 'Look, the man has become like one of us, knowing good and evil. Now, so that he does not reach out his hand and also take from the Tree of Life and eat and live forever—' the LORD God sent him out from the Garden of Eden to work the soil from which he had been taken. So he drove the man out, and in front of the Garden of Eden he stationed cherubim and a flaming sword, which turned in every direction to guard the way to the Tree of Life" (Genesis 3:22-24). With their ouster from the Garden of Eden, Adam and Eve were separated from the Tree of Life and therefore had to physically die at some point. Moreover, messengers from God separated them from the place where they had met with the holy God. Without a mediator, they could no longer directly approach God because they had lost his image.

The LORD Created a People for His Plan

God's promise to Eve opened the door to salvation for all people. St. Paul wrote, "This is good and pleasing in the sight of God our Savior, who wants all people to be saved and to come to the knowledge of the truth" (1 Timothy 2:3,4). God's desire, however, would have been frustrated if he had not taken concrete steps to carry out the plan and to communicate it to the people of the earth. From eternity God has been thorough. His plan of salvation therefore contained means using his creative power both to carry out the plan and to arrange circumstances for communicating the plan to humankind.

We do not have mention or evidence of human communication via well-developed forms of writing during the early the history of the world. Information was passed orally from one person to another. As we know from when we have tried to pass a message through a series of people by word-of-mouth, the message often becomes garbled. While we do not know why God decided to grant his early human population much longer lives than people have today, his decision did help prevent the message of his salvation from being lost. Early people were able to relate what God had done and promised, not just to their children or their grandchildren, but to their descendants six or eight generations after them.[5] Because the length of human life, like other human characteristics, is controlled by the genes in people's DNA molecules, God can thereby adjust the human lifespan for his purposes. Following the flood, God began using his creative power to shorten the human lifespan in the same timeframe that writing became more common.

When people became so sinfully repulsive that God could not stand them, he decided he had to act. The LORD said, "I will wipe out mankind, whom I have created, from the face of the earth, along with the animals, the creeping things, and the birds of the sky, because I regret that I have made them" (Genesis 6:7). That the animals were also punished by God's destruction shows how man's corruption also extended to everything living. Because the LORD wanted to fulfill his promise of salvation, however, he called a man to be the conduit for the line of his Savior by creating a way for him to survive the destruction God would impose on the rest of mankind. "Noah was a righteous man, a man of integrity in that generation. Noah walked with God…So God said to Noah,…'Make an ark of gopher wood….'" (Genesis 6:9-16). Through Noah and the ark, God moved his plan of salvation forward. Noah, of course, was not righteous of himself but was righteous in the sight of God because he believed God's promise of the Messiah.

Sometime later God brought his plan to rescue man into sharper focus. He chose a particular family to be the ancestors of the Savior whom he would send. The man God called to head this family was a Semite[6] named Abram, whom he later renamed Abraham.[7] He moved Abram westward from Mesopotamia to Canaan and guided him through a set of trying experiences to grow his family. He promised Abraham that his family would be the bearer of the Messiah[8] and gave him the covenant of circumcision. God said, "This is my

---

[5] See Genesis 5, which gives the lifespans of Adam and his early descendants. We do not know if these genealogies are complete, so it would be unreliable to attempt to calculate the age of the Earth from them as Bishop James Ussher did in AD 1650.

[6] Semites are descendants of Noah's son Shem.

[7] God metaphorically describes his selection of the family of Abraham in Ezekiel 16:3-14. It was a selection completely from grace, not from the grandeur of the progenitor of the race.

[8] [God said,] "All of the families of the earth will be blessed in you." (Genesis 12:3b)

God's Re-Creation of Man

covenant, which you shall keep, a covenant between me and you and your descendants after you: Every male among you shall be circumcised" (Genesis 17:10). God also made a covenant with him in which he assured Abraham that his family would eventually receive the land of Canaan as their inheritance. God promised to arrange events so this would happen. God continued his management of events for Abraham's son Isaac, for Isaac's son Jacob (whom he renamed Israel), and for Israel's twelve sons, who were collectively the ancestors of the children of Israel. On his deathbed, Israel bequeathed the line of God's promised deliverer to Judah (Genesis 49:10). The account of Abraham and of his family occupies much of the book of Genesis.

After allowing the Israelites to grow into a nation, first in relative isolation in Canaan and then while in slavery in Egypt over a period of 400 years, God called Moses to be the prototype of a deliverer for the people of Israel (Exodus 3:1-4:17.). God performed a series of miracles through Moses and his brother Aaron to bring the people out of Egypt and shepherd them to Canaan. During the journey God gave them his law to train the Israelites, and he created the objects and events that were needed to bring them safely through the wilderness. Moses and Joshua, his successor, led Israel, God's chosen people, into the earthly home that God had promised. This was intended to symbolize the heavenly home to which he would eventually lead all believers in his promise.

For the good of our own souls, we must recognize there was nothing special about the people of Israel that caused God to choose them and to put up with their insolence while he rescued them from slavery. Moses wrote, "For you are a people that is holy to the LORD your God, because the LORD your God has chosen you to belong to him as a people that is his treasured possession…The LORD became attached to you by love and has chosen you, not because you were more numerous than all the people. Actually you were the fewest of all the peoples" (Deuteronomy 7:6,7). God's plan of grace for mankind relied on his almighty power, not on the strength of his agents.

The LORD Created a Path for His Messiah[9]

Through the hands of Moses and Joshua, God effected the rescue of his people from physical slavery and brought them into an earthly promised land.

---

[9] Eggert, *Simply Lutheran*, pp.81-168.

It was more urgent, however, for him to bring them into an appropriate spiritual relationship with himself. Because he was holy, he could not allow even his chosen people to think they could just waltz into his presence any time they wanted. They too were sinners, and they needed to repent. God therefore chose to work with them through mediators. These mediators were the members of the tribe of Levi. Aaron and his sons were made the priests, men who would intercede and make atonement for the people (Exodus 28:1). The rest of the Levites would instruct the people and assist in the duties involved in tabernacle and temple worship (Deuteronomy 31:10-13; Numbers 4:21-33).

After the leadership of the priests had proven to be a mixed blessing, God gave Israel kings. In particular, he called David to be the shepherd of his people, but he also identified David's family as the family that would bear the promised deliverer from Satan. God told Nathan the prophet to say to David, "Your house will stand firm, and your kingdom will endure forever before you. Your throne will be established forever" (2 Samuel 7:16). That Redeemer would, like David, become the king of Israel. However, his rule would be over a spiritual Israel rather than over a physical Israel. David understood the unique role that God had given him, and he recognized it was all by God's almighty power that he, the eighth son of a poor family, could be given such phenomenal blessings. From this point, God would no longer subdivide the line through which the Savior would pass. The Messiah would always be referred to as a "son of David."[10]

Once the LORD had confined the line of the Savior to David's family, he was ready to permit a temple to be built for himself (1 Kings 5:1-9:5). This temple would be God's earthly home, where people could always come to meet with him through his designated mediators. In this way God created a visual reminder that he had made a promise and that he would always be there to fulfill his promise. As the cloudy pillar in the wilderness had reminded the people of the LORD's presence on the way out of Egypt, so the temple would always remind the people their all-powerful God dwelled among them. Above the atonement cover of the Ark of the Covenant was where he wanted his people to seek him through his appointed mediators.

The priests and the kings were not always faithful to the LORD, so he called men, and occasionally women, to deliver his message boldly. He created visions and dreams through which they received revelations from him to relay to the kings, the priests, or the people. These divinely called prophets were

---

[10] Matthew 1:1.

sometimes given the ability to work signs to demonstrate that their messages came from the LORD and not from themselves. God could create changes in nature for the purpose of creating changes in hearts. Even so, true prophets' words were always in harmony with the Scriptures as they had been recorded up to that point. Isaiah wrote, "To the law and to the testimony! If people do not speak according to this word, there will be no dawn for them" (Isaiah 8:20).

Sadly, God's words through the prophets were not heeded, so the LORD sent his people into exile—first the northern kingdom of Israel and then Judah. "God sent prophets among them to bring them back to the LORD. The prophets testified against them, but they did not listen" (2 Chronicles 24:19). Exiling the people of captured nations was a common practice at the time. It prevented the exiled people from reorganizing and resisting their conquerors. Such exile was meant to disperse and forever break the cohesiveness of conquered peoples. When Judah was sent into exile, its people feared that the nation of Judah would never rise again. However, God used his creative power to put into the mind of the king of Persia a disposition to return the Jewish exiles to their homeland and to reestablish both their capital of Jerusalem and their temple to serve the LORD. "In the first year of Cyrus king of Persia, in order to fulfill the word of the LORD that came by the mouth of Jeremiah, the LORD stirred up the spirit of Cyrus king of Persia, so that he made a proclamation throughout his kingdom and put it in writing" (2 Chronicles 36:22). On the other hand, God made certain the rebuilt city of Jerusalem and the rebuilt temple were not as glorious as the originals, perhaps so the returnees would recognize both that rebellion against the LORD had a cost attached to it and that their deliverance would not come through their earthly kingdom. "However, when many of the older priests, Levites, and heads of families, who had seen the first house, saw this house being founded, they wept loudly." (Ezra 3:12a).

The LORD Sent His Promised Redeemer

After the LORD returned the Jews from exile in Babylon, he soon fell silent. The Jews were left to read his promises and to wait for the fulfillment of his pledge to redeem them. It was a long wait of nearly 400 years during which political strife seemed to accomplish nothing. Yet, God created out of this strife and uncertainty the societal environment he desired for his intervention into history to introduce his promised Messiah. St. Paul wrote, "When the set time had fully come, God sent his Son to be born of a woman, so that he would be born under the law, in order to redeem those under the law, so that we would be adopted as sons" (Galatians 4:4,5).

The fulfillment of the promise began with the miraculous announcement of the forthcoming birth of a son to the aged priest Zechariah (Luke 1:5-25). God's creative power was at work striking Zechariah mute for his unbelief and creating the life of his messenger John the Baptizer in the womb of a woman past childbearing age. Zechariah's imposed silence was not broken until his son had been born. He then burst into a song created in his heart by the Holy Spirit (Luke 1:67-79). John the Baptizer was the fulfillment of the prophesy that God would send someone in the spirit of Elijah to prepare the way for his Redeemer of mankind.[11]

The stage was set for God's greatest creation. Through the action of the Holy Spirit, the Son of God, the second person of the Trinity, was incarnated, that is, combined with human flesh, and was humbled by being placed in the womb of a lowly virgin.[12] The eternal, infinite God thus united with a finite, temporal body of flesh to become one being! We do not know how this was accomplished, and many nominal Christians refuse to accept what the Bible tells us about what God did. "Mary said to the angel, 'How will this be, since I am a virgin?' The angel answered her, 'The Holy Spirit will come upon you, and the power of the Most High will overshadow you. So the holy one to be born will be called the Son of God....For nothing will be impossible for God'" (Luke 1:34-37). The power of God is indeed limitless in doing what is necessary to carry out his will. The Bible tells what God did, and we would be calling God a liar if we doubted what he has done. The miracle of miracles—two natures, one person—capable of doing any action that God himself could do but also able to feel and sense all the things that a human could feel and sense. He filled the space and time of the universe while also being present in the space of a circumscribed human body at a definitive point on the terrestrial timeline. Reason rebels at the idea, but faith trusts the word of the LORD. To

---

[11] [The LORD said,] "Look! I am going to send Elijah the prophet to you before the great and fearful day of the LORD comes! He will turn the hearts of fathers to their children and the hearts of children to their fathers." (Malachi 4:5,6a)

[12] Harlyn J. Kuschel, *Christ*, People's Bible Teaching Series (Milwaukee: Northwestern Publishing House, 2007).

Koehler, *Christian Doctrine*, pp. 133-145.

God's Re-Creation of Man

reassure us, the writer to the Hebrews recorded, "Therefore, since the children share flesh and blood, he also shared the same flesh and blood, so that through death he could destroy the one who had the power of death (that is, the Devil) and free those who were held in slavery all their lives by the fear of death" (Hebrews 2:14,15).

As a human being, Jesus, this God-man, was under the same law of God that all other people are under (Galatians 4:4). That was formalized at his circumcision, where his human blood was first shed so he could become part of God's chosen people as other Jewish boys. As truly a human, Jesus had to face the same temptations all other humans have had to face, but he did not fall to the temptations like Adam and Eve had. "One [Jesus] who has been tempted in every way, just as we are, yet was without sin" (Hebrews 4:15b). In fact, he had to face a greater degree of temptation because Satan realized who he was and the importance of disrupting God's plan of salvation (Matthew 4:1-11). Yet this being, who combined the eternal Son of God with the nature of a human, was up to the task of resisting all the devil could throw at him. This accomplishment is referred to as Christ's "active obedience" because he actively worked to keep the law that no human had previously been able to keep.

Nonetheless, the active obedience of the Messiah was not enough to save us. Only Jesus would have enjoyed God's eternal bliss based on his obedience if the issue of all human sin was not addressed. The sins of every person separated that person from approaching God for inclusion in his kingdom. Unless the guilt of a person's sins were atoned for, i.e., paid for, God's judgment of eternal damnation would be a certainty. As a psalmist wrote, "Therefore the wicked will not stand in the judgment, nor sinners in the assembly of the righteous" (Psalm 1:5), and St. Paul declared, "For the wages of sin is death" (Romans 6:23a). God therefore created a situation in which Jesus was accused of blasphemy for claiming he was God, and he was beaten, mocked, spit upon, and crucified. His crucifixion was a horrible punishment, but Jesus had to endure much more. He had to endure God's punishment for the guilt of the sins of all the humans who were living, had lived, and would live. Only the God-man could endure such punishment and survive. And he did survive. He did not give up his human life until he had finished his redemptive work. Only then did his human soul depart from his human body. This is called Christ's "passive obedience" because he subjected himself to the punishment of his Father.

But God had not finished his creating work in support of his plan of salvation. God re-created life in the human body of Jesus. His human soul returned, and he rose from the dead. As the first words of the book of Galatians read, "Paul, an apostle—not from men, nor through a man, but through Jesus Christ and God the Father, who raised him [Jesus] from the dead" (Galatians 1:1). Death could not hold the God-man who, even in death, possessed all the powers of the omnipotent God. The resurrection, however, only masked the greater creation of God. Because the guilt of all the sins of all mankind had been paid for by the death of Jesus, the LORD created a way to transfer the righteousness of Christ's perfect life to every human, making them righteous before God.[13] St. Paul wrote, "That is, God was in Christ reconciling the world to himself, not counting their trespasses against them" (2 Corinthians 5:19a). Sins paid for and righteousness imputed—the curse of sin Adam and Eve had brought on mankind had been removed by God's fulfillment of the promise he had made to our first parents immediately after they had committed their act of rebellion. The Creator had his perfect creature back.

The LORD Sent His Spirit

Had God ended his creative work at this point, every human being would still have gone to hell. They would have been justified, by what we call "objective justification," but they would not have known that God had granted this pardon for their sins. They would have remained slaves to sin rather than stepping forth as children of God. God needed to bring the knowledge of his salvation to all people and then create faith in their spiritually dead hearts to believe his decree of redemption. The task of bringing the people to receive this saving message, that is, effecting "subjective justification," was assigned to the Holy Spirit. Jesus commanded those who already believed to spread the word. People could not believe what was unknown to them. St. Paul wrote, "So then, how can they call on the one they have not believed in? And how can they believe in the one about whom they have not heard? And how can

---

[13] Wayne D. Mueller, *Justification*, People's Bible Teaching Series (Milwaukee: Northwestern Publishing House, 2002).
Koehler, *Christian Doctrine*, pp. 201-210.

God's Re-Creation of Man

they hear without a preacher?" (Romans 10:14) Yet, it was only the Holy Spirit, being God himself, who had the power to create faith.[14]

Finally, a simple knowledge of the facts of God's plan of salvation, i.e., a "head knowledge," is not enough to save people from hell. A new person must be created by the Holy Spirit within everyone who will be saved. The creation of this new person will lead the converted soul to repent of all his or her sins because the new person hates sin just as God hates sin. The new person will also want to do good works to serve God, not to earn salvation, but out of pure joy and thanksgiving for being redeemed and converted to faith. St. Paul wrote, "As far as your former way of life is concerned, you were taught to take off the old self, which is corrupted by its deceitful desires, and to be renewed continually in the spirit of your mind, and to put on the new self, which has been created to be like God in righteousness and true holiness" (Ephesians 4:22-24). This work of the Holy Spirit within us is called "sanctification,"[15] and it continues for our whole lifetime.

The LORD created the world, he created man, and he re-created man after man had polluted the world through his rebellion against his loving God. Yet, God's creative work on behalf of man was not done at that point. There is still the matter of death. God redeemed man from the necessity of enduring eternal death in hell through the work of the Son of God in his active and passive obedience to the will of his Father. God the Holy Spirit rescued man from spiritual death, which allowed him to receive the free pardon that permits him to enter heaven. But there remains physical death, which has been slaying people since the time of Abel. To live with God forever in heaven requires that the bodies of all people be raised from the dead and that a new realm be created where believers will dwell. These activities will be the subject of the next chapter.

---

[14] John M. Brenner, *Conversion*, People's Bible Teaching Series (Milwaukee: Northwestern Publishing House, 2000).

Koehler, *Christian Doctrine*, pp. 185-191.

[15] Lyle W. Lange, *Sanctification*, People's Bible Teaching Series (Milwaukee: Northwestern Publishing House, 1999).

Koehler, *Christian Doctrine*, pp. 211-216.

9

Judgment – The End of the Creation

As stated in chapter 6, God did not tell us what would have happened if man had not sinned. Would earth have in some form or another been man's eternal home or would God at some point in time have transferred man to another realm? We cannot know and we do not care. With the fall of man, God implemented his plan of salvation that will end with the elect[1] living in paradise with God. We have seen that this plan is well on its way to completion. In this chapter we will soar with Jesus, the prophets, and the apostles as they preview the almighty power of God that he will use to finish what he began in Genesis 1.[2]

The Day of the LORD

The children of Israel were aware the earth was only their temporary home. A psalmist wrote, "Your years go on through all generations. Long ago you laid a foundation for the earth, and the heavens are the work of your hands. They will perish, but you remain. All of them wear out like a garment. Like clothing you will change them, and they will be changed. But you are the same, and your years will never end. The children of your servants will dwell with you, and their descendants will be established before you" (Psalm 102:24-28). The psalmist tells us that God used his creative power to establish the physical world and that he will use it to end the physical world. The days

---

[1] The elect are those who were included in the Decree of Predestination in chapter 2.
[2] Thomas P. Nass, *End Times*, People's Bible Teaching Series (Milwaukee: Northwestern Publishing House, 2011).
Koehler, *Christian Doctrine*, pp. 395-425.

of everything, not just people, are numbered. The earth will wear out and lose its usability, but the LORD will preserve his people after the earth is no more.

The LORD revealed the same view of the earth's future to Isaiah. "Lift up your eyes to the heavens. Look closely at the earth beneath, because the heavens will vanish like smoke, and the earth will wear out like a garment, and its inhabitants will die like gnats. But my salvation will remain forever, and my righteousness will never be abolished" (Isaiah 51:6). The substance of the earth that we have come to rely upon as God's agent to give us what we need to live and thrive will grow old and vanish. The physical universe is temporary, but God's salvation will carry us through the destruction of this world. Already 700 years before the Messiah was born, the faithful in Israel understood this. The people were not surprised when Jesus talked about the end of the world.

The day when the earth will be destroyed became known as the "Day of the LORD." The LORD tried to be very clear about what would happen. In an oracle he told Isaiah, "Look, the Day of the LORD is coming, a cruel day, with wrath and fierce anger, a day to make the land desolate, a day to destroy its sinners there. For the stars of the sky and its constellations will not give their light. The sun will be darkened as it rises, and the moon will give no light. I will punish the world for its evil, and the wicked for their guilt. I will put an end to the arrogance of the insolent, and I will humble the pride of the ruthless" (Isaiah 13:9-11). The Day of the LORD will be dreadful, but some of the Jews believed that judgment would only apply to their enemies. God therefore sent a message through Amos saying, "Woe to those who long for the Day of the LORD! What good will the Day of the LORD be for you? It will be darkness and not light" (Amos 5:18). The practice of taking the clear Word of God and distorting it to justify one's own belief is nothing new.

The number of times the Day of the LORD is mentioned in the prophets surprises many people who have been led to believe this is a New Testament concept. In addition to the references above, the Day of the LORD is mentioned in Isaiah 2:12 and 34:8, Jeremiah 46:10, Lamentations 2:22, Ezekiel 7:19, 13:5, and 30:3, numerous times in Joel 1 and 2, Obadiah 15, and in Zephaniah 1-3. Some of these references list events that will occur on the Day of the LORD. For example, Joel wrote, "For the Day of the LORD is near in the Valley of Decision. The sun and moon will be darkened, and the stars will stop shining" (Joel 3:14,15). In all, eight prophets wrote about the Day of the LORD, with Jeremiah including it in both his books (Jeremiah and Lamen-

Judgment – The End of the Creation

tations). Sometimes the phrase was used in terms of a severe local punishment inflicted on the people for their sins, but more often it was a reference to the severe final judgment on those who reject the LORD and do not repent. Malachi closed the last book of the Old Testament with both a prophecy of the promised salvation beginning with a special messenger from God but also with a prophecy of utter destruction for those who fail to heed the words of the messenger. Malachi wrote, "Look! I am going to send Elijah the prophet to you before the great and fearful day of the LORD comes! He will turn the hearts of fathers to their children and the hearts of children to their fathers. Otherwise, I will come and strike the land with complete destruction" (Malachi 4:5,6).

Before the advent of the prophets, the phrase "the Day of the LORD" does not appear in the Bible. This does not mean, however, that God did not regularly during the earlier period of Israel's history make promises of divine aid for his people coupled with promises of divine judgment upon his people. In that era, God was training his people how to be faithful by using the more short-term promises about the physical environment of Israel. He used this as a symbol of the eternal promised land. When God decided the people of Israel were ready to view a bigger picture of his plan of salvation, the prophets became more urgent in writing about God's mercies and judgments on all mankind. All these passages from the prophets made clear that when the Day of the LORD arrived, God was going to use the same power he used to create the world to uncreate it, that is, to rearrange the elements of his creation or to destroy them.

Jesus Prophesied Judgment Day

The phrase "the Day of the LORD" in the Old Testament was not completely comprehended by all who used it. The people of Israel came to understand there would be punishment for the enemies of God's people, but the prophets further indicated the evildoers among God's people also had something to fear. In the New Testament, the expression and the concept of this great day when the LORD would come to administer justice remained, but the format of the day as Judgment Day with Jesus as judge was brought more clearly into focus.

Jesus began his warnings by indicating the period before the day of judgment was rapidly shortening. He said, "I must do the works of him who sent me while it is day. Night is coming when no one can work" (John 9:4). It will be day as long as the gospel can be preached, but the ability to preach that message will end when Judgment Day comes. In the parable of the ten virgins (Matthew 25:1-13), Jesus urged people to always be ready, for they did not know when he would return to judge the world. He noted, "No one knows when that day and hour will be, not the angels of heaven, not even the Son, but only the Father" (Matthew 24:36). There will be no advance warning. It is tragic so many people throughout history have tried to prove Jesus a liar by attempting to establish the day of his return.

Jesus furthermore made clear Judgment Day would be no natural phenomenon. He said, "Immediately after the misery of those days [i.e., days of turmoil on earth], the sun will be darkened, and the moon will not give its light; the stars will fall from the sky, and the powers of the heavens will be shaken. Then the sign of the Son of Man will appear in the sky. And at that time all the nations of the earth will mourn. They will see the Son of Man coming on the clouds of the sky with power and great glory. He will send out his angels with a loud trumpet call, and they will gather together his elect from the four winds, from one end of the heavens to the other" (Matthew 24:29-31). St. Luke noted Jesus also said, "And on the earth nations will be in anguish, in perplexity at the roaring of the sea and the surging waves, people fainting from fear and expectation of the things coming on the world" (Luke 21:25,26a). When the Day of the LORD comes, the God who created the universe will begin destroying that universe. The works of the fourth day of creation (Genesis 1:14-19) will be undone. The components of the universe will no longer obey the "laws of nature" as they did when the promise of the LORD that "seedtime and harvest" would endure was still in effect (Genesis 8:22). God will then re-create the world for his courtroom scene where Jesus will judge the nations. Jesus said, "When the Son of Man comes in his glory, and all the angels with him, he will sit on his glorious throne. All the nations will be gathered in his presence, and he will separate them one from another, as a shepherd separates the sheep from the goats" (Matthew 25:31,32).

The Apostles Reaffirmed Jesus' Prophecy

The apostles also described Jesus' return as a time when God will use his creative powers to alter key elements of the world he had made. On the day

Judgment – The End of the Creation

of the first Pentecost after Jesus ascended to heaven, St. Peter quoted the prophet Joel saying, "I will show wonders in the sky above, and signs on the earth below, blood and fire and a rising cloud of smoke. The sun will be turned to darkness and the moon to blood before the coming of the great and glorious day of the Lord. And this will happen: Everyone who calls on the name of the Lord will be saved" (Acts 2:19-21).

The apostles were particularly strong in echoing Jesus' warning about being prepared for his return in power and glory. St. Paul wrote, "Concerning the times and dates, brothers, there is no need to write to you, for you yourselves know very well that the day of the Lord will come like a thief in the night. When people are saying, 'Peace and security,' destruction will suddenly come on them, like labor pains on a pregnant woman, and they will certainly not escape" (1 Thessalonians 5:1-3). St. Paul even filled in details about the sequence of events on Judgment Day. "For the Lord himself will come down from heaven with a loud command, with the voice of an archangel, and with the trumpet call of God, and the dead in Christ will rise first. Then we who are alive, who are left, will be caught up in the clouds together with them, to meet the Lord in the air" (1 Thessalonians 4:16,17a). The full power and majesty of God will be on display as those long dead will spring to life. St. Peter also stressed there will be a sudden display of God's supernatural power when he wrote, "But the day of the Lord will come like a thief. On that day the heavens will pass away with a roar, the elements will be dissolved as they burn with great heat, and the earth and what was done on it will be burned up. Therefore, since all these things will be destroyed, what kind of people ought you to be, living in holiness and godliness, as you look forward to and hasten the coming of the day of God?" (2 Peter 3:10-12a). St. Peter continued by underscoring the horrifying sight as God uncreates the stage on which the drama of man had played out, "That day will cause the heavens to be set on fire and destroyed, and the elements to melt as they burn with great heat. But according to his promise we look forward to new heavens and a new earth, in which righteousness dwells" (2 Peter 3:12b,13).

In writing the book of Revelation, St. John restated the two key points God desired man to know about the end of the world. First, the LORD will use his almighty power to bring his Genesis 1 creation to an end and to bring all people to judgment before his Son Jesus. St. John wrote, "Then I saw a great white throne and the one who sat on it. The earth and the sky fled from his presence, and no place was found for them. I also saw the dead, great and small, standing in front of the throne, and books were opened. Another book was also opened, which is the Book of Life. The dead were judged by the things written in the books, according to what they had done. The sea gave up the dead that were in it, and Death and the Grave gave up the dead that were in them, and they were judged, each one according to what he had done" (Revelation 20:11-13). Second, the LORD will create a new place for his elect to dwell. "Then I saw a new heaven and a new earth, because the first heaven and the first earth had passed away. And the sea no longer existed" (Revelation 21:1).

There has been a disagreement among theologians for centuries concerning whether God will completely destroy the current universe and create the "new heaven and new earth" out of nothing (*ex nihilo*) or whether after purging the universe of its evil, he will reshape it into the new home for mankind. The Bible does not give us enough information to resolve this issue. Therefore, it is unimportant that we know what God will do. We are dealing with the Lord God Almighty here, and he will do what he knows to be best no matter how strong an argument we advance that he should handle matters differently.

The creation saga began in Genesis 1 with God forming the current heavens and earth out of nothing, and it will conclude at the end of Revelation with his destruction of his first creation and with his creation of a new heaven and a new earth. It is the account of God's creative power being used from the beginning to the end for the benefit of mankind, his perverse and rebellious creature. How could there be greater love than what God showed in his actions revealed in the Bible? Our study of God's creative work is complete with this chapter. In the next four chapters we will examine how we should and should not react to it.

10

Creation and the Lutheran Confessions

We believe all the doctrines of Christianity solely because the Bible reveals them to us. If something is not revealed in the Bible, then it has no bearing on our salvation. It is an irrelevant matter, and we do not teach it as doctrine. Whether it is true or false does not affect our faith. As Lutherans, we say we believe in the principle of *sola scriptura*, from the Scriptures alone. This being the case, it might seem our study of creation should have ended with the last chapter. Yet, we not only need to believe what the Bible teaches, we must be ready to state clearly what we believe. St. Peter wrote, "Always be prepared to give an answer to everyone who asks you to give a reason for the hope that is in you" (1 Peter 3:15b). Because there will continually be people who promote their own ideas as God's will and try to distort the Bible to support such ideas, it sometimes becomes necessary to formally state the scriptural position and present appropriate biblical quotations to support it. Such situations in the past led to the formulation of the Lutheran Confessions, just as they led to the writing of this book.

The Lutheran Confessions,[1] which are contained in the Book of Concord, are ten documents that were developed to address specific challenges to the Christian faith. At any point in history, some doctrines might be in dispute, while numerous other doctrines might generally be accepted by all members of a Christian group. At such a time a confession might be drafted to clearly state the biblical teachings being challenged, but that confession would likely not mention or only nominally refer to the generally accepted doctrines. For

---

[1] All quotations from the Lutheran Confessions, including the creeds and catechisms, used in this book are taken from Paul T. McCain, ed., *Concordia: The Lutheran Confessions*, A Reader's Edition of the Book of Concord, 2nd ed. (St. Louis: Concordia Publishing House, 2006).

example, confessions drafted in defense of the biblical doctrines against Roman Catholic teachings did not devote much space to the doctrine of the Trinity because both sides agreed on that doctrine. The important issue in drafting a confession is that, as we have been warned against in the book of Revelation, it does not add to or subtract from what the Scriptures teach. "I give this warning to everyone who hears the words of the prophecy of this book: If anyone adds to them, God will add to him the plagues that are written in this book. And if anyone takes away from the words of the book of this prophecy, God will take away his share in the Tree of Life and in the Holy City, which are written in this book" (Revelation 22:18,19). Because the Lutheran Confessions teach what the Scriptures teach, we subscribe to (i.e., accept) them *quia*, which means "because," not merely *quatenus*, which means "in so far as," they agree with the Scriptures.

God's creation of the world was not a point in contention in the eras when the confessions contained in the Book of Concord were developed. God's creation of the world was generally accepted; consequently, not all the confessions speak of or even allude to God's creating activities. The references they make to creation are part of their discussion of other matters.[2] Nevertheless, these references are important. They show that the Lutheran commitment to the biblical teachings on creation was the same when the Book of Concord was drafted as are being presented in this book.

The Ecumenical Creeds

The Lutheran church accepts three creeds that are referred to as "ecumenical" because they are used throughout Christendom. This is somewhat of an overstatement because only the Nicene Creed is regularly used by all Christians who use creeds in their worship services. Nonetheless, the teachings in the three creeds are nominally accepted by all Christian churches, even though not all use them in their liturgies.

The Apostles' Creed is the first creed contained in the Lutheran Confessions. It was developed from the baptismal confessions employed in early Christian congregations when adult converts were baptized. It has been used in Western Christian churches, particularly around Rome, since the second century. It states, "I believe in God, the Father Almighty, maker of heaven and earth." This sentence firmly declares a personal belief in the divine crea-

---

[2] Nafzger, *Confessing the Gospel*, vol. 1, pp.151-161.

tion of the universe.³ The Apostles' Creed expresses the faith of the apostles, but it was not written by the apostles. It is not used in the liturgies of the Orthodox churches.

The Nicene Creed was initially developed by the First Ecumenical Council that met in Nicaea in AD 325 in what is now Turkey. It was finalized by the Second Ecumenical Council that met in AD 381 in Constantinople, which is now Istanbul. The central purpose of these meetings was to refute the Arian heresy, which claimed the Son of God was God's first creation and not God from eternity. The Nicene Creed is the second creed in the Lutheran Confessions. In its final form it reads, "I believe in one God, the Father Almighty, maker of heaven and earth and of all things visible and invisible."⁴ This sentence clearly states that the individual members of the Christian church believe in the teachings of Genesis 1. To combat the Arian heresy, however, the creed continues. "And in one Lord Jesus Christ, the only-begotten Son of God, begotten of His Father before all worlds, God of God, Light of Light, very God of very God, begotten, not made, being of one substance with the Father, by whom all things were made." This clearly denies the Arian heresy and agrees with what was presented previously in chapters 2 and 3 of this book.

The Athanasian Creed, like the Apostles' Creed, is a creed of the Western church and not in general use in the Orthodox churches. It was composed in southern France about the beginning of the sixth century. It was named for Athanasius, the Patriarch of Alexandria, Egypt, who was a great defender of trinitarian Christianity at the time of the First Ecumenical Council. The creed declares the Father, the Son, and the Holy Spirit are individual persons of the Trinity and are all eternal, infinite, and uncreated. Together these persons compose the Godhead, and they have no independent existence.⁵ The relation-

---

3   Edward Schlink, *Theology of the Lutheran Confessions*, trans. Paul F. Koehneke and Herbert J. A. Bouman (Philadelphia: Fortress Press, 1961), pp. 37-66, 226-69.
4   Lutheran hymnals sometimes have "we" instead of "I" in their statement of the Nicene Creed, but both the German and the Latin versions of the creed in the Book of Concord have the word for "I."
5   For example, Jesus said, "But if I am doing them, even if you do not believe me, believe the works so that you will know and understand that the Father is in me, and I am in the Father" (John 10:38) and "When the Counselor comes, whom I will send to you from the Father—the Spirit of truth, who proceeds from the Father—he will testify about me" (John 15:27).

ship among the persons is discussed in chapter 2 to the extent that it is known. In this creed the church confesses that because each person is eternal, infinite, and uncreated, they were all present when the creation of the world was begun in Genesis 1:1, as discussed at the beginning of chapter 3. Therefore, this creed affirms God was not created in whole or in part but that the world was created by God.

The Large and Small Catechisms

In 1529, Martin Luther released both his Large Catechism and Small Catechism to the printers, and they became instant successes. They are still in use today. The Small Catechism has been amplified by the addition of questions, answers, and Bible verses to Luther's explanations. The goal of these books was and still is to present the chief parts of the Christian faith in a manner so Christians without advanced theological training can understand and apply these biblical teachings to their daily lives. There is no specific article in these catechisms that discusses creation, but creation is referenced frequently either directly or indirectly throughout them.

We will consider the Small Catechism first. Reference to God as the Creator already appears in Luther's explanation to the first article of the Apostles' Creed.[6] Luther's answer to his question on the meaning of this article begins "I believe that God has made me and all creatures. He has given me my body and soul, eyes, ears, and all my limbs, my reason, and all my senses, and still preserves them." This is not only a clear affirmation of God's creation of the initial world, but it is also a declaration that God is continuing to create with each new generation. Not only people as entire beings but also the individual parts of each of us are crafted by God. Luther continued, "In addition, He has given me clothing and shoes, meat and drink, house and home, wife and children, fields, cattle, and all my goods. He provides me richly and daily with all that I need to support this body and life." Here Luther switched from God's creative power being used to call beings and objects into existence to the use of his creative power to sustain them. Whatever good we receive comes exclusively from God. Finally, Luther pointed out God additionally blesses us with safety. "He protects me from all danger and guards me and preserves me from all evil." Luther confessed by these words that the LORD not only provides us with goods but also protects us from every harm the hosts of hell might inflict

---

[6] The Apostles' Creed is the second "chief part" in Luther's Small Catechism.

upon us while we live in this world. Luther concluded, "He does all this out of pure fatherly, divine goodness and mercy without any merit or worthiness in me." In chapter 6 we saw the LORD continued to work for the benefit of mankind even after human beings had destroyed God's perfect world. Luther stated the same thing here. The LORD's love for mankind was so great that he continued to use his creative power to sustain this race of rebels. Jesus remarked, "For he [God the Father] makes his sun to rise on the evil and the good and sends rain on the righteous and the unrighteous" (Matthew 5:45b).

In explaining the fourth petition of the Lord's Prayer,[7] Martin Luther wrote that "daily bread" was "everything that belongs to the support and needs of the body, such as food, drink, clothing, shoes, house, home, fields, cattle, money, goods, a pious spouse, pious children, good government, good weather, peace, health, honor, good friends, faithful neighbors, and the like." Yet, the spoken petition is only "Give us this day our daily bread." When we pray this petition, we are asking God to use his creative powers for our benefit and to sustain our lives by appropriately arranging the things of nature. Praying for such things if we did not believe the LORD could do whatever was necessary to provide them for us would be hypocrisy. St. James wrote, "But let him ask in faith, without doubting, because the one who doubts is like a wave of the sea, blown and tossed by the wind. In fact, that person should not expect that he will receive anything from the Lord" (James 1:6b,7). Praying the Lord's Prayer therefore confesses God as the Preserver of creation.

Considering Luther's explanation of the first article of the Apostles' Creed and of the fourth petition of the Lord's Prayer, we can understand why he started all his explanations for the meanings of all the commandments[8] after the first with "We should fear and love God so that...." Because God has created for us everything we need, we are to use these gifts of God as he intended them to be used. Our parents are to be honored because God created us from them.[9] We are to regard human life as precious because God created it.[10] We are to regard marriage as inviolate because God gave it as part of his crea-

---

[7] The Lord's Prayer is the third "chief part" in Luther's Small Catechism.
[8] The Ten Commandments is the first "chief part" in Luther's Small Catechism.
[9] I have depended on you since I was in the womb. You separated me from my mother's body. (Psalm 71:6)
[10] [God said,] "In fact, I will hold each animal and each person responsible for your lifeblood. I will hold each man responsible for the life of his brother." (Genesis 9:5)

tion.[11] We are to respect our neighbor's goods because God gave these created things to our neighbor.[12] We are not to speak falsely because God created our voices to praise him.[13] We are not to covet our neighbor's property because God will create enough to satisfy our needs.[14] Since God is the great Creator of everything, Luther insisted God had the right to give us these commandments.

We also find references to God's creative work in the Large Catechism. In discussing the Apostles' Creed as an entirety, Luther wrote, "God has created us for this very reason, that He might redeem and sanctify us" (LC II.64).[15] As was discussed in chapter 6, man was God's purpose from eternity for the creation of the universe. The three articles of this creed show the activities of all three persons of the Godhead in carrying out his purpose from the start of his creation. Luther's understanding of this was critical to his theology.

In LC I.133, Luther explained the promise that is attached to the Fourth Commandment as more than a *quid pro quo* deal with God. The phrase "that you may live long on the earth" is not just a matter concerning years of life but rather a divine promise concerning the quality of life that God will provide. Luther pointed to St. Paul's statement "that it may go well with you and that you may live a long life on the earth" (Ephesians 6:3). God controls the environment in which we live and can adjust it so it is best for our eternal salvation, but his plan may also involve enhanced temporal blessings for us.

In LC II.13-16, Luther explained everything God did, no matter how great or how small, is wrapped up in the word "Creator." We have the list of blessings from article I of the Apostles' Creed in the Small Catechism, but Luther added even more detail in the Large Catechism. He wanted us to realize we

---

[11] For this reason a man will leave his father and his mother and will remain united with his wife, and they will become one flesh. (Genesis 2:24)

[12] If you come upon your enemy's ox or his donkey going astray, you certainly must bring it back to him again. If you see that the donkey of someone who hates you has fallen down under its load, do not pass him by. You certainly must help him with it. (Exodus 23:4,5)

[13] St. James warned about misusing the tongue when he wrote, "With it we bless our Lord and Father, and with it we curse people, who are made in the likeness of God." (James 3:9)

[14] [Jesus said,] "So do not worry, saying, 'What will we eat?' or 'What will we drink?' or 'What will we wear?' For the unbelievers chase after all these things. Certainly your heavenly Father knows that you need all these things." (Matthew 6:31,32)

[15] LC II.64 is a shorthand representation used in the Book of Concord to mean the Large Catechism, Section II (the Apostles' Creed), paragraph 64. Paragraphing may differ among languages and translations, but the relative location marked by the numbers in the text remains the same. Each confession has its own abbreviation (AC - Augsburg Confession, Ap - Apology to the Augsburg Confession, Ep - Epitome of the Formula of Concord, SD - Solid Declaration of the Formula of Concord).

Creation and the Lutheran Confessions

need to keep our blessing list open for even more additions. Our lives and our welfare are served by creatures great and small that God has provided and by the inanimate agents, such as water and the sun, which he has also created. We can manage these, but it is God who owns them. In the paragraphs that immediately follow in the Large Catechism, Luther also reminded us that we cannot see all the things that God has created for us. Some, like the air, are invisible but are essential to our existence. Some, like the angels, are supernatural and protect us from evils that we do not even realize are threatening us. Some, like good government and peace, are ethereal. We cannot grasp them, but they are still creations of God to serve man, his special creature. For all these creations of God, we ought to thank him and to use them for his glory.

Luther returned to the benefits that God has created for us through civil authorities in the fourth petition of the Lord's Prayer (LC III.73-75). When there is tranquility, it is easy for us to forget the good God carries out through our governments. Luther urged those to whom God has entrusted the care of the state to remember that they must labor for the common good. Although we ultimately receive everything we have from God, good government permits these blessings to flow to us uninterruptedly. Both rulers and their subjects need to remind themselves of this often. We need to pray for our government officials.

As is often true in studying Luther's theology, we need to return to his understanding of the first commandment. To Luther the First Commandment was the cornerstone of the law. While the law cannot save, our understanding of the law allows us to see our sin and to recognize how our new man can serve his Savior. In LC I.26-28, Luther reminded us we must worship God alone because all good things come from him who can give to us much more than we can imagine.[16] Nevertheless, God often works through agents that we realize can be either the laws of nature or the creatures that serve as God's physical hands. Yet, we should not permit these agents to obscure our sight of our ultimate benefactor. It is our Creator God whom we are to worship and thank for all the gifts we receive. Moreover, we should act as his agents to spread his goodness to others.

---

[16] Now to him, who is able, according to the power that is at work within us, to do infinitely more than we can ask or imagine. (Ephesians 3:20)

The Unaltered Augsburg Confession and the Apology

The Augsburg Confession was written by Philipp Melanchthon in 1530 for presentation to the Holy Roman Emperor Charles V at the Diet of Augsburg.[17] After the Roman Catholic theologians wrote the Confutation to refute the Augsburg Confession, Melanchthon wrote the far more detailed Apology to the Augsburg Confession[18] the following year. Because these confessions were prepared so soon after Luther's catechisms were written and because Luther was the unseen hand behind these documents, it is natural there was some carryover of expression between them.

Article I of the confession states, "He [God] is the maker and preserver of all things visible and invisible" (AC I.2). This article is entitled "God" and reaffirms the first article of the Nicene Creed. It continues, "These three persons [Father, Son, and Holy Spirit] are of the same essence and power" (AC I.3). This statement denies the Arian heresy by avowing that God the Son was not an inferior or created being. AC I.5&6 mention heretical groups whose teachings the Lutheran theologians rejected because they did not recognize the existence of God the Son or regarded him as a created deity of lower rank than God the Father. With these statements the signers of the confession made clear they accepted the equality of the persons of the Trinity and that God is a separate entity from his creation.

The article entitled "Original Sin" begins "Our churches teach that since the fall of Adam, all who are naturally born are born with sin" (AC II.1). This sentence recognized God's creation of Adam recorded in Genesis 2 and his fall into sin recorded in Genesis 3. Adam's sin was the reason for God's rescue plan for mankind, which is the basis of the rest of the Scriptures. The early inclusion of Adam's fall in this key document not only confessed creation but also God's response to sin, which is discussed throughout the Confession. This article of the Confession used the term "concupiscence," i.e., "a strong desire," to describe original sin and to show that it is no small matter. The Apology reads "Scripture testifies to this [the image of God that was lost in the fall] when it says in Genesis 1:27 that man was made in the image and likeness of God" (Ap II.18). Here the creation of man was specifically referenced as being within the first six days.

---

[17] Because Melanchthon subsequently massaged the language in the Augsburg Confession to permit Reformed theologians, such as John Calvin, to sign it, the use of the phrase "unaltered" has become common to indicate the original confession.

[18] That is, a defense of the Augsburg Confession.

The article entitled "The Son of God" testifies, "Our churches teach that the Word, that is, the Son of God, assumed the human nature in the womb of the Blessed Virgin Mary. So there are two natures—the divine and the human—inseparably joined in one person" (AC III.1&2). The statement confesses God's great creation that united the eternal and the temporal into one person. It is beyond comprehension what God's creative power can do. We cannot explain it, but we believe it, as did our spiritual forefathers, because God said it.

In defending Article IV entitled "Justification," the Apology declares, "Such faith is not an easy matter, as the adversaries dream. Neither is it a human, but it is a divine power" (Ap IV.250). Faith is a creation of God within our hearts. While we must do the believing, it is the Holy Spirit that puts the faith there and preserves it against the hosts of hell. This is also stated in the Confession itself. "Through the Word and Sacraments, as through instruments, the Holy Spirit is given. He works (creates) faith, when and where it pleases God in those who hear the good news" (AC V.2). When God makes something new where there was nothing or only something old, he creates.

The Augsburg Confession was presented to Emperor Charles V in both German and Latin, with Electoral Saxony Chancellor Dr. Christian Beyer reading it in German before the Diet. The German version of the confession is therefore regarded as the original document. This normally matters very little, but it does in Article XVI entitled "Civil Government." The Latin version is less forceful in confessing that "all governments are created and put in place by God" (AC XVI.1). The German version much better reflects what Luther wrote in his catechism, namely, that governments are creations of God as a conduit for God's blessings. The article explains that because governments are created as agents of God, Christians can participate in government by holding positions of responsibility but must also obey the government except when the government directs them to sin.

Finally, the creative work of God is referenced regarding marriage. Article XXIII of the Apology, entitled, "The Marriage of Priests," attacks the Roman church's rule preventing priests, monks, and nuns from marrying. The Apology bases its argument on the creative work of God. "Genesis 1:28 teaches that people were created to be fruitful, and that one sex should desire the other in a proper way" (Ap XXIII.7). The Apology continues "This love of one sex for the other is truly a divine ordinance." The Apology thus firmly traces its argument back to the creation. "Human nature is so formed by God's Word that it is fruitful not only in the beginning of creation, but as long as this nature of our bodies exists. Humanity is fruitful just as the earth becomes fruitful by the Word, 'Let the earth sprout vegetation, plants yielding seed' (Genesis 1:11)" (Ap XXIII.8).

The Formula of Concord

The Formula of Concord was developed through a long process involving many of the most gifted Lutheran scholars of the later sixteenth century. It was an essential endeavor to reconcile Lutherans to each other and to prevent the Lutheran church from fragmenting and the work of Martin Luther from being lost to future generations. After a series of manuscripts were drafted, the Lutheran theologians and the Lutheran rulers agreed on a document entitled the "Formula of Concord," which contained a detailed "Solid Declaration" and a summary called the "Epitome." While most of the articles in the Formula deal with issues involving God's plan of salvation, the first article entitled "Original Sin" heavily referenced creation theology.

The reason for this article was the Flacian Controversy. In a theological debate with a defender of synergism,[19] Matthias Flacius had overstated the biblical position on original sin and claimed it was the very substance of the human soul. This raised two questions. First, was God creating sin as he created new souls for people at their conception? Second, how could souls be redeemed if they themselves were original sin? Even more troubling, if sin is the substance/essence of a human soul, then either Jesus was not human, or he was a sinner. In either case, he could not be our Savior. In drafting Article I of the Formula, the Lutheran theologians rejected Flacius' argument by appealing to the divine creation. They wrote, "God created not only the body and soul of Adam and Eve before the fall, but also our body and soul after the fall….and still recognizes them as his work" (Ep I.4). To address the problem of purifying the human nature of its incredible corruption, they wrote, "Only the new birth and renewal of the Holy Spirit can and must heal this deranged, corrupted human nature" (SD I.14). These writers' commitment to God as the Creator was therefore three-fold—God had directly created our first parents,

---

[19] Synergism is the teaching that man must cooperate with God to some degree to be saved. There are several forms of synergism, depending on where in the conversion or preservation-of-faith process the cooperation appears.

he still creates all human beings, and he creates new spiritual life in those who are being saved.

The Lutheran confessions strongly and in many ways affirm God's initial creation of the universe and his continual creation through his acts of preservation and through his bringing forth of new life in this world. Our spiritual forefathers indeed accepted divine creation without reservation. Additional examples from the confessions could be cited, but it is time to proceed to a discussion of science, a current challenger to many people's belief concerning God's creation.

11

Science and Theology

Whenever we undertake a new task, we need to learn the rules and requirements governing that task so we can perform it properly. If we desire to become dental assistants, we need to know the various aspects of healthy and diseased teeth, the procedures for cleaning teeth, and the use of personal protective equipment. If we desire to work on a railroad operating crew, we need to know the hand and whistle signals, the meaning of timetable entries, and the rules for train priority. For us to do either job requires substantial technical training to prevent injury to health and property.

In the same way, if we want to play specific games or sports, we must know the rules and strategies for them. For example, four people can play hearts or bridge with a 52-card deck by dealing hands of thirteen cards. How the hands are evaluated and played, however, is completely different in these two games. We would not pass three cards to the left in bridge or use a dummy in hearts. We would be interested in the number of tricks we could take in bridge, but we would want to avoid taking tricks with points in hearts. Moreover, understanding the nuances of each game is essential to playing it well.

If we are to be successful, we must perform professional tasks or play games within the rules governing them. A dental assistant who does not protect a patient properly when taking x-rays may increase the risk of cancer. A switchman who does not reset a switch to the main line after use may cause a derailment. A card player who plays a card illegally will be penalized in the scoring or excluded from future games. Part of our personal maturing process is learning to work and play within the rules so we can live together as a community.

The Nature of Theology

Christian theology is the search for and proclamation of the truth about God and his plan of salvation for mankind. It is based completely on divine revelation. But how do we determine if something is true? For truth to have any meaning it must be testable against a standard. Without a standard, the validity of any statement is in doubt. If we worked for a railroad, we would regularly consult *The Consolidated Code of Operating Rules*.[1] If we are playing cards, we might consult *Hoyle's Official Rules of Card Games*.[2] If all of us are not all working or playing by the same rules, we will not be able to determine whether a particular operation or behavior is proper and legal. For example, the rules for what constitutes a legal catch of a forward pass differ between college and professional football. Similarly in theology, we must establish a standard by which to judge statements that people claim to be true or false. We call this standard "hermeneutics."

There are three factors in playing card games—the rules of the game, the cards in a player's hand, and the strategy employed by the player. Players with the same cards playing under the same rules might use different strategies and therefore obtain different results. In fact, this is the whole purpose of duplicate bridge tournaments in which numerous players at different tables who are all playing the same hands get different results based on their strategies. In theology, however, we want all people who are interpreting a specific passage or studying a specific doctrine to get the same results, that is, reach the same conclusion about its meaning. That is the whole purpose of establishing the biblical interpretation principles we call "hermeneutics." Unlike a game where the rules and strategies are separate entities, however, hermeneutics functions as both the rules for and the strategy of interpretation. Therefore, if the same portion of Scripture is studied by the same hermeneutics, the same interpretation will always result. Here we see the difference between how common activities with which we are familiar work and how biblical interpretation functions. This is necessary groundwork for understanding the similarities and differences between theology and science.

---

[1] *The Consolidated Code of Operating Rules*, Edition of 1980 (Printed by each railroad).
[2] *Hoyle's Official Rules of Card Games*, Deborah Doyle, ed. (New York: Broadway Books, 2000).

The study of hermeneutics is outside the scope of this book, but a presentation of it at the layperson's level is available elsewhere.[3] Some key principles of Lutheran hermeneutics are: 1) The Scriptures are the inerrant, verbally inspired Word of God, 2) Scripture rather than reason must be used to interpret Scripture, 3) unless indicated otherwise by the text, the text must be taken literally, 4) clear passages are used to understand less clear passages, and 5) each doctrine has an unambiguous passage teaching it that is called a *sedes doctrinae* (seat of doctrine). The first of these principles is sometimes called the "fundamental assumption of biblical theology." When these hermeneutic principles are applied, theologians and general readers of the Bible separated by both centuries and different cultures will come to the same interpretation of the various passages of the Bible.

Before looking at how science handles truth, we must be aware of three practical points concerning biblical interpretation. First, the Bible does not change. There will be no new evidence to cause people to reach a different conclusion about spiritual truth. We say that the "canon" of the Bible is closed, that is, it contains all God's revelation. Second, while portions of old manuscripts are occasionally found, such as the Dead Sea Scrolls, these finds have not altered a single doctrine.[4] Moreover, sometimes additional contextual information is found from an era or a location in which a part of the Bible was written. While this information occasionally allows us to better identify animals or objects or to better understand how things were done, they also have not changed a single doctrine that God has revealed in the Bible. God has watched over the integrity of his Word because his Word is one of his means of grace. Finally, some people corrupt biblical hermeneutics by introducing human reason or non-biblical principles that permit them to interpret the Scriptures more to their liking. For example, John Calvin introduced the principle of "the absolute sovereignty of God in all matters." This non-scriptural principle led him to falsely conclude that all unbelievers were predestinated to be damned, thereby denying God's desire to save all mankind as described in chapter 8.

---

[3] Eggert, *Simply Lutheran*, pp. 21-38.
[4] Eggert and Kieta, *Clearing a Path*, pp. 215-221.

The Nature of Science

It is surprising to many people to learn there are many similarities between the methods of theology and the methods of science. Like theology, science is looking for truth. Like theology, science has a fundamental assumption and a methodology (hermeneutics) that unite the rules and the strategy science uses to search for truth. Before we consider the different types of science and what limits them in their pursuit of truth, we need to examine the parallels between theology and science. We begin by recognizing that while theology is based strictly on the revelation in the Bible, the framework of science is inductive reasoning as it is applied to the universe. In inductive reasoning a small sample of the members of a population[5] is analyzed, and then a model is formed to generalize what has been observed to the whole population. This approach must be used whenever the members of the population are too numerous to permit analysis of each member individually.

As explained above, the fundamental assumption of biblical Christianity is that "the Bible is the inerrant, verbally inspired Word of God." The fundamental assumption of the natural sciences (i.e., the physical and biological sciences) is that "all observations of natural phenomena can be explained in terms of the inherent properties of matter, energy, space, and time."[6] We note that both these approaches to seeking truth have a clearly stated standard of truth, but their standards are radically different. Theology relies solely on God's revelation in his Word, which is completely known to us. Science relies solely on the properties of matter, energy, space, and time, which are to a large extent not yet known and which must be learned over time by experimentation. Scientific truth will therefore change as new discoveries are made, but Bible-based theological truth will never change.

Additionally, the evidence used in theology and science has different characteristics. All the evidence used to study theology is already completely present in the Bible. It is available to everyone today, and it has been available for many centuries. In contrast, new scientific evidence is continually being discovered. New methods of gathering evidence are regularly being devised. Scientific evidence is also affected by the nature of what is being studied. Much of the massive amount of evidence in the physical sciences is of high quality

---

[5] A population could be a group of people, rocks, stars, atoms, or anything that has some similarity.
[6] Robert M. Hazen, *The Joy of Science*, The Great Courses, (Chantilly, Virginia: The Teaching Company, 2001), Lectures 1,2.

and was collected under strict rules of evidence. The collection of high-quality evidence in some but not all areas of the biological sciences is impeded by the inability of scientists to isolate what is being measured from its environment. Experiments often cannot be exactly duplicated, and the elimination of all experimenter and subject bias in systems using human subjects can be difficult. Similar factors make gathering reliable evidence in some social sciences even more challenging. The quality of the evidence must always be considered when evaluating a scientific model, and such evaluation frequently requires a significant technical background.

Next, we must consider how the hermeneutics of theology and science are employed. Application of Lutheran hermeneutics to the Scriptures is a systematic process that involves identifying all the possible meanings of each word and phrase in the original languages for a selected passage. The process then compares that passage with other passages on the same topic to make certain that if there is more than one possible meaning, the correct meaning has been chosen. Consultation with current scholars and reading documents showing how previous generations of scholars understood the passage are also important to prevent self-deception. The final decision on meaning can then be used in teaching the general membership of the church. The understanding that results from this process is called "theological truth" or "biblical truth."

Scientific hermeneutics is called the "scientific method." Evidence is carefully gathered and validated and then compared with other evidence to facilitate the identification of patterns. Explanations of these patterns are subsequently formulated into models (i.e., theories) to explain what has been observed. Once the models have been constructed and tested, they are placed before other scientists in what is called the "falsification challenge." Due to the complexity of many areas of science, this challenge is critical to filtering out misunderstandings and bad ideas. It may lead to the rejection of the proposed model or its modification, but if the model passes this test, it is provisionally accepted and used in teaching and as the basis of further research. The result of this process is called "scientific truth." Because this book contains both theology and science, it has been placed before both theologians and scientists in its review process.

The major difference between theology and science in the matter of the interpretation of evidence is that the source of theological information, namely, the Scriptures, does not change. That means biblical scholars for many centuries have studied the same material and their conclusions serve as a bulwark against false ideas. Conversely, new evidence in science is continually being produced or discovered. Therefore, scientists who did not have this new evidence in the past might have drawn conclusions that are no longer valid in the light of currently available information. For this reason, all scientific theories can only be accepted provisionally. New evidence may cause them to be revised or replaced with better theories at any time.[7] While the biblical interpretation is stable,[8] with nuances only based on how it should be applied in the current world environment, theories of science are always in flux. Certainly, some scientific models are much less likely to be affected by new evidence than others, but no scientific model can be accepted with absolute certainty.

Even without referring to specific examples that we will study in the next chapter, it should be obvious there is a difference between theological truth and scientific truth. Theological truth rests on an unchanging base of evidence, while scientific truth rests on a shifting base of evidence. Theological truth comes through divine revelation, while scientific truth comes from the often-limited ability of man to gather evidence about nature. Theological truth was revealed to man to make him wise unto salvation. Scientific truth is sought to improve the temporal living conditions of humanity and to satisfy inherent human curiosity. That error-prone human methodology would produce the same conclusions as error-free divine revelation is hardly to be expected.

Reason versus Logic

Both theologians and scientists must deal with the general confusion that exists between reason and logic. "Reason" is based on philosophy, and "logic" is based on deductive reasoning. Let us consider deductive reasoning first.

Deductive reasoning defines (creates) a "domain" by giving it a set of rules, elements, and operators. Because each domain is defined by us as its human creators, we have forced every statement we can make about that do-

---

[7] Martin Sponholz, "Two Towers" Minnesota District Pastoral Conference, Minneapolis, April, 1982, http://essays.wisluthsem.org: 8080/handle/123456789/3836.

[8] False doctrine occurs in the church when people allow their reason to override the honest application of biblical hermeneutics because they do not like what such a study of Scriptures reveals. All of us are tempted to fall for Satan's query "Did God really say…?" (Genesis 3:1) when we wish God would have spoken otherwise than he did.

Science and Theology 125

main to be either absolutely true, absolutely false, or indeterminable. For example, let us consider a domain consisting of different-sized blocks. If Block A is larger in size than Block B, and Block B is larger in size than Block C, then Block A is larger in size than Block C. If Block D is larger than Block B, then it is also larger than Block C, but we do not have enough information to determine if it is larger than Block A because no relationship has been established between Block D and Block A. In the domain of the integers, 2 plus 3 is always equal to 5, 6 minus 8 is never equal to 3, and 0 divided by 0 is undefined, i.e., indeterminable. In deductive reasoning we cannot learn anything not established by the definitions used to create the domain. Mathematics and logic, which are examples of deductive reasoning, are used in both theology and science without creating difficulties.[9]

"Reason" is a philosophical term that is not based on deductive reasoning or inductive reasoning, and this can cause confusion. Reason in the philosophical sense, when applied to theology or science, means drawing a conclusion based on whether something makes sense to the human mind.[10] For example, that Christ can be one person composed of both a divine nature that is infinite in its attributes and a human nature that is finite in its attributes does not make sense to the human mind. Therefore, some people violate the principles of Lutheran hermeneutics by trying to develop a solution their minds find "reasonable." Such an approach subjects divine revelation to human rationalization. The same problem occurs in science. Because an electron is a fundamental particle,[11] it is hard to understand how it can have a delocalized presence in an atom. Various atomic models are used to rationalize the electron's behavior for non-scientists. Many phenomena in quantum physics (e.g., quantum entanglement) and in cosmology (e.g., black holes) are so bizarre to human thinking that our efforts to explain them accurately may be compromised by our inclination to make them rational. *Neither in his revelation in his Word nor in his structuring of his creation is the LORD required to be rational by human standards.* A psalmist wrote, "The LORD does whatever

---

[9] The use of deductive reasoning in science is shown by the block example. An example of its use in theology is "because all people have been declared righteous before God, therefore I have been declared righteous before God."

[10] What makes sense to one human mind does not necessarily make senses to everyone else's human mind.

[11] An electron is a fundamental particle of particle physics, at least according to our current model.

he pleases in the heavens and on the earth, in the seas and in all the depths" (Psalm 135:6).

The confusion between the use of logic and the use of reason arises from the failure of people to appropriately define the domain in which they want to apply logic. As previously stated, logic can never be used to learn information that is not inherent in the domain established by the definitions creating it. Drafting those definitions so they are consistent with the known evidence is essential. If that is not done, then our logic is not sound, and we slide into the realm of philosophy. Because there are no standards of truth universally accepted in philosophy, false conclusions can easily be drawn. In theology, these are called "heresies." In science, these lead to wasted time and effort as scientists try to validate what is, in fact, false. Historically, this type of false science dates to Aristotle, who believed all natural processes were rational and could be understood through careful analysis instead of experimentation. It was not until the time of Galileo that experimentalists began pushing philosophers out of their dominant position in the physical sciences.[12] The struggle has not yet ended, however, because in the less rigorous sciences and in the minds of dreamers, many ideas without legitimate evidence are pushed forward, particularly when the undereducated public can be duped into supporting the charlatans.

The Roots of the Dispute over Creation

The fundamental assumption of any system for seeking truth sets in place various logical conclusions arising from that assumption. It is, in effect, the cornerstone of the domain in which truth will be sought. The fundamental assumption of biblical theology is that the Bible is the inerrant, verbally inspired Word of God. If this assumption is true, then we must draw our conclusions about how the world came into existence based on what we find in the Bible. As we saw in chapters 3 and 4 of this book, the answer comes quickly because the first chapter of the Bible states very clearly the LORD created the world in six days, and that message is reinforced by God's statement to the same effect from Mount Sinai before more than a million witnesses.[13] The

---

[12] For example, Aristotle claimed that the speed at which objects fell was proportional to their weight because that seemed philosophically reasonable to him. Galileo proved experimentally that objects fall at the same speed.

[13] [God said,] "For in six days the LORD made the heavens and the earth, the sea, and everything that is in them." (Exodus 20:11)

Science and Theology 127

first nine chapters of this book document in substantial detail this conclusion based on what the Bible reveals concerning the world's origin. There is no doubt what the Bible asserts about creation, and the truth of that assertion is independent on whether one believes it. There is no wiggle room in what we can understand from the biblical revelation.

The fundamental assumption of the natural sciences is that all observable phenomena can be explained in terms of the inherent properties of matter, energy, space, and time. If this assumption is true, then there are no supernatural beings that can interfere with the laws of nature, which are anchored in the inherent properties of matter, energy, space, and time. If supernatural beings do exist, they are without power in the physical world and are effectively nonentities. This is a forced conclusion (i.e., a logical corollary) of the fundamental assumption of science. Furthermore, since according to this assumption nothing can interfere with the operation of the laws of nature, the universe must have reached its current state of being through the actions of the laws of nature. In other words, it must have evolved because there is no logical alternative in the physical universe as constrained by the fundamental assumption of science. Note that science thus proves evolution not by observation or experimentation but as a logical conclusion from its fundamental assumption that constrains the domain in which science operates.[14] Moreover, scientists constrain their domain in this manner for purely practical purposes. If their fundamental assumption were not made, then it would be impossible to determine whether any observed phenomenon of nature was the result of natural processes or of the intervention by a supernatural being. This situation would make all scientific explanations of nature meaningless. Experimental verification could not be done because scientists could not be certain that God did not to some degree "have his finger on the scale" and was not in some way influencing what they observed. Without an assumed relationship between cause and effect, engineering and medicine could not be practiced, and modern society could not exist.

Therefore, the disagreement between science and theology over the origin of the universe is rooted in conflicting fundamental assumptions that underlie

---

[14] Note that the fundamental assumption of science does not "establish" the domain in which science works because that domain is the physical universe. Rather the assumption "constrains" how the evidence from the physical universe can be interpreted.

the domains in which they operate. Simply put, they have different definitions of what constitutes evidence that can be used to establish truth. Both fundamental assumptions cannot be true; one or both must be false. Because of this, it is impossible to resolve whether the universe was created or evolved. The evidence each side produces is not regarded as valid by the other side. It takes faith to believe the fundamental assumption of either side. The faith of the disciple of biblical Christianity is created by the Holy Spirit. The faith of the disciple of science is rationalized from the promptings of the human mind to understand the universe and to master it. These promptings go back to Eve wanting to be like God and the people of Babel wanting to build a tower to the heavens.

Science and Scientists

In the final section of this chapter, we will consider the different types of science and who are legitimate scientists. The terms "science" and "scientists" are often used and misused in the media and among the untrained public. Let us begin by considering the different types of science and what limits their application. All science involves observations of nature. In some cases, there is nothing more we can do besides observe, such as when we see a hurricane sweeping across the Gulf of Mexico. When we are limited to only observing events that occur naturally, we say we are practicing "observational science." On the other hand, sometimes we can make changes and observe the effects of those changes on the behavior of some aspect of nature, such as when we drop stones of various sizes from the same height. When we can perform observations based on changes we make, we are practicing "experimental science."

Experimental science itself can be divided into two types. One type is called the "hard sciences," such as analytical chemistry, where it is possible to isolate the entity being studied (e.g., calcium ions) from its environment, thereby eliminating interferences. The experiments can be exactly duplicated by others with similar equipment, thereby removing experimenter bias and providing an easy way to falsify[15] incorrect theories or results. The second type is called the "soft sciences," such as pharmacology, where researchers cannot completely isolate the entity being studied (e.g., drug metabolism)

---

[15] "Falsify" used in this manner by scientists means to prove something false, not to make it false.

from other factors (e.g., emotional stress). Repeating experiments may yield significantly different results because the other factors cannot be exactly duplicated. This means scientific truth in the soft sciences cannot be as reliable as it is in the hard sciences.

By contrast, in observational sciences, such as astronomy, scientists are limited by what they can find in nature. They can search where they hope to find new or confirmatory information, and they can study what they do find with the best methods available. Nevertheless, they cannot generate new cases to study. For example, astronomers cannot create planets or galaxies to enable them to test their models. Although the reliability of observational science research is generally much less than that of experimental science, its results are often overstated in the media. Lack of reproducibility and the difficulty in establishing legitimate falsification challenges are significant issues for purely observational sciences. While all scientific models are somewhat fragile and susceptible to being overturned by new discoveries, scientific truth in the hard sciences is much more reliable than in the soft sciences and much more testable than in the observational sciences.

Even when science is practiced correctly with the best equipment and methods, three logical issues still prevent scientific truth from being anything more than provisional. This is because science is based on inductive reasoning, and these logical issues (i.e., fallacies) are an inherent property of inductive reasoning.[16] Let us explore them.

First, the assumptions made by scientists in studying a phenomenon might be false.[17] False assumptions can distort the conclusions drawn from the evidence and thereby invalidate the theories built on that evidence. For example, for a long period of time it was falsely assumed by everyone that all heavenly bodies orbited the Earth. Of greatest importance, if the fundamental assumption of science is false, all theories, no matter how sound they appear, are uncertain and their scope of usability undeterminable. This applies to all evolutionary models. The existence of the almighty God makes science's fundamental assumption false.

---

[16] Eggert and Kieta, *Clearing a Path*, pp. 25-28.
[17] This logical fallacy is called "false premise."

Second, as previously mentioned, new evidence may invalidate established theories.[18] For example, Newton's laws of motion were replaced by those of Einstein and other physicists because certain observations could not be explained in the Newtonian model.

Third, just because a theory perfectly accounts for all results does not mean it gives the right explanation for their occurrence.[19] For example, suppose someone theorized that the sun rises because roosters crow early in the morning and wake it up. No matter how much evidence is gathered in support of this theory, it is still false. All science suffers from this problem because correlation does not prove causation.

The three issues given above limit the validity of every form of science. Because they are inherent problems of inductive reasoning and not problems of methodology, they will never go away. Scientific research has discovered a vast amount of useful information that has led to great improvements in engineering, medicine, and agriculture, and it should not be disrespected. Nevertheless, scientific truth is limited because of the inductive reasoning environment in which science is forced to be practiced.

Science, of course, is the practice of legitimate scientists. Not everyone who puts on a lab coat is qualified as a scientist. To be a research scientist, one must accept the fundamental assumption of science as a working hypothesis, even if one does not regard it as absolute truth. One must have a broad and deep knowledge of at least one and preferably several scientific fields. One must do research, have the educational background to design and evaluate experiments, publish articles about the research in respected scientific journals, and be regarded as competent and honest by other scientists. Furthermore, one must be objective regarding the outcome of experiments and the validity of scientific models. In many ways, a good scientist is similar to a good theologian, merely working off a different fundamental assumption.

Unfortunately, numerous people who consider themselves to be scientists or allow people to believe they are scientists do not meet these qualifications. One group is composed of those who do not have sufficient education, training, or research experience. For example, many people consider physicians, engineers, and other technical people to be scientists. While certainly a few are, the great majority of them are well trained only to practice in their

---

[18] This logical fallacy is called "hasty generalization" where the conclusion is drawn on too little evidence.
[19] The logical fallacy here is called "affirming the consequent."

technical field and to understand the relevant journals, but they do not have the training or experience to do research in it.

A second mislabeled group contains those who have the appropriate training and experience but who have become advocates for particular ideas rather than honest researchers. For example, companies often hire such "scientists" to produce data to support their corporate agendas. In other cases, such as that of the famous chemist Linus Pauling,[20] they become spokesmen for causes in which they do not have expertise.

Third, most science teachers, regardless of the level at which they teach, have at least some education in the sciences but are not scientists, except at research universities or top-rated teaching colleges. In fact, in elementary and secondary schools, a science field might not have been a science teacher's educational major. Finally, there are the technical writers who present science to the public in a way that gives the impression they really understand it but whose shallow knowledge often misleads rather than educates the public. Such people cause most research scientists to shudder.

Even qualified and dedicated scientists are human, and they can deceive themselves and others. The falsification process, introduced above, was designed to help scientists stay honest. In the physical sciences, where large numbers of researchers have similar instrumentation, no one can risk publishing defective data because someone else will certainly try to duplicate what has been claimed. The fear of public disgrace keeps people honest. In medical research, when possible, "double blind" studies are done. When this is done, the experimental medicine and the placebo are identically packaged and coded so that neither the researcher nor the subjects know who is getting the real drug. Only after the experiment is completed does a referee release the identity of those who had been given the drug of interest. Scientists must constantly be careful so 1) their controls are similar enough to their research samples to prevent control bias, 2) their samples are representative of the population being studied, and 3) the statistics they are applying are appropriate for their methodology. There are many scientists who produce high-quality research by meticulously following these practices.

---

[20] Linus Pauling was an American chemist of the twentieth century who invented valence-bond theory and was the only person to win two unshared Nobel prizes. He became an advocate for using mega-doses of vitamin C to prevent the common cold.

The qualitative difference in the evidence and models of the various branches of science is significant, but there is a general respect among scientists that each is doing the best he or she can under the natural and technical limitations of their respective scientific fields. This can lead scientists in the more rigorous sciences to treat the models produced in less rigorous fields of science (see chapter 12) with higher regard than is merited by the evidence that can be gathered to support them. In particular, this can cause those in the hard sciences to give more credence to evolutionary models in other fields than may be warranted due to the limitations that scientists in the less rigorous fields face in collecting and validating their evidence.

With the background laid by this chapter, we are ready to discuss proper creation apologetics. In the next chapter we will look at how to defend the teachings of the Bible by showing they are just as well-grounded and credible as the models created by evolutionary scientists. Everything goes back to the fundamental assumptions and those inherent limitations of science because science is forced to work using inductive reasoning.

12

Creation Apologetics

Apologetics is not about winning arguments. Its purpose is to show the position we hold is a logically sound position given the assumptions we have made and given the evidence based on those assumptions. In our defense of our faith, we show that our assumptions are as reasonable as those of people who hold other views and that the evidence they present does not disprove what we believe. Through this approach, we attempt to gain respect for our position and blunt our opponents' attacks on it. To accomplish this, we do not ridicule our opponents or question the honesty of their work. We do not misstate their position to make a strawman we can easily knock down. We respond to the best of their arguments, not dwelling on any obvious mistakes they have made while trying to present their position.

The beliefs of biblical Christians are under continual attack from many quarters. Other books deal with various of these attacks and should be consulted when making a defense of our faith in these areas.[1] In this chapter we will restrict our apologetics to some common threats to the biblical teachings about creation.[2] In previous chapters we have already considered some apologetic arguments, which we will expand upon here. We will consider additional topics as well and look at challenges based on the type of science involved. It is important, however, we remember what was presented in the last chapter,

---

[1] Eggert and Kieta, *Clearing a Path*.

Mark A. Paustian, *Prepared to Answer* (Milwaukee: Northwestern Publishing House, 2004).

Mark A. Paustian, *More Prepared to Answer* (Milwaukee: Northwestern Publishing House, 2004).

[2] Arthur A. Eggert, "Creation, Science, and Our Approach in Apologetics," *Wisconsin Lutheran Quarterly*, Vol. 112, No. 4 (Fall 2015), pp. 252-278.

namely, that scientists are not trying to prove evolution. They have concluded the universe came about through large-scale evolutionary changes as a corollary of their fundamental assumption, not based on their scientific investigation. Their research merely attempts to determine how evolution happened, not whether it happened. Let us begin by looking at some necessary background information.

Background Science

All matter is composed of elements. Each atom, the smallest unit of an element, has a nucleus that contains an integer number of protons, called the atomic number, and an integer number of neutrons. All atoms of the same element have the same number of protons but can have differing numbers of neutrons. Each unique arrangement of protons and neutrons is called an "isotope." Elements are arranged sequentially in a "periodic table" by atomic number, and they are limited in number by the amount of positive charge a nucleus can hold without fragmenting. Most isotopes are radioactive and decay into other isotopes, emitting radiation until they reach a stable (i.e., non-radioactive) isotope. The length of time for radioactive isotopes (called "radioisotopes") to decay to undetectability is based on first-order kinetics[3] and the precise characteristics of their nuclei.[4] This decay time is unique for each radioisotope, never changes, and can be determined precisely. Decay times range from much less than a second to billions of trillions of years.[5]

Two methods exist for using radioisotopes directly to determine how old something is.[6] Method one is based on measuring the ratio of the amount of a radioisotope of a specified element present to the total amount of that element present in the object of interest. This ratio decreases as time passes because the radioisotope decays. If we know this ratio for an object at the time that it was formed and measure the ratio now, we can place these two numbers into the first-order decay formula and compute how much time has elapsed since

---

[3] In first-order kinetics, the rate of decrease of a substance is proportional to the amount of that substance present. After one time interval the amount is reduced to half its initial value, after two intervals to one-quarter, after three intervals to one-eighth, etc.

[4] Nuclear decay is traditionally described in terms of its half-life; the time it takes for a given amount of a radioactive isotope to decay to half that amount. It takes about 15 half-lives for radioisotopes to decay to non-detectability.

[5] Most radioisotopes do not exist naturally on Earth, but they can be created in nuclear reactors.

[6] Eggert and Kieta, *Clearing a Path*, pp. 112-114.

Creation Apologetics 135

the object came into existence. That gives us the apparent age of the object. This is the method used in dating with carbon-14.[7] This method is unreliable if we cannot be certain of the ratio of the radioisotope to the total of that element originally present, which is often the case for carbon-14 dating. Carbon-14 is formed by the collision of cosmic rays with nitrogen-14 high in the atmosphere. If the conditions in the atmosphere were somewhat different in the past, then we would not know what the starting ratio of carbon-14 to total carbon had been in the object of interest, and our calculated time would be inaccurate. To eliminate this problem, a calibration curve can be created by measuring the carbon-14 ratios in objects whose ages are known from historical data and then comparing the ratio measured in the object of interest whose age is sought with that curve. Unfortunately, this approach limits the method to being useful only for objects from the last several thousand years for which we have reference substances of known age.

In method two we sum the current amount of the radioisotope present and the current amount of the product isotope present, both of which we can determine by chemical analysis. We use this sum as the initial concentration of the radioisotope in the decay equation. This method gives very reliable results (error < 1%), provided that there was no product isotope in the object when it formed and that no product isotope escaped from it later. Fortunately, the two uranium-to-lead decay series that are most frequently used to date rocks and other ancient items are not affected by either of these problems.[8] The existence of two long-lived uranium isotopes that decay by different pathways provides an internal check on the results. While the radioisotopes of other elements are not as versatile, highly developed analytical procedures made their use quite reliable. Method two cannot be used for carbon-14 dating because the decay product of carbon-14 is nitrogen-14, which is ubiquitous, making up almost 78% of the atmosphere.

An unrelated but important issue to be aware of is how distance is measured in space. The distances to the closer stars have been calculated by using their slightly different positions in the sky as the Earth moves through half of its orbit around the sun. By this trigonometric calculation, we find the nearest

---

[7] Carbon-14 contains 6 protons and 8 neutrons. Most carbon is stable carbon-12, with 6 protons and 6 neutrons. There is a small amount of stable carbon-13.

[8] Lead, the decay product, does not readily fit into the crystal structure of uranium compounds when they are formed, and it cannot escape later, since it is not a gas.

star is 25,000 trillion miles away. Numbers of this size can be daunting, so we divide them by the distance light travels in one year (5,879 trillion miles) to give more manageable numbers, in this case 4.3 lightyears. Although light travels incredibly fast, it does not travel instantaneously, so we cannot see any event from which the light has not yet reached us. Moreover, we see things as they were when the light left them, not as they are now.

Physics – The Age of the Earth

As noted in chapter 3, the Bible does not give us the exact age of the Earth; therefore, we do not have a precise number to defend. Nevertheless, we can deduce from the Bible that the age of the Earth is in the range of thousands of years, not millions or billions of years. This conclusion is drawn from how the Bible uses exact ages and how it structures genealogies. The LORD placed great emphasis on the lineage between the man who first sinned and the Savior whom God sent to save mankind from the consequences of sin. That lineage is outlined in Luke 3:23-38. While not all the ancestors in the lineage are listed, the presentation of the lineage shows a clear purpose in linking Adam and Jesus. Some of those missing can be placed into the lineage based on information given in other parts of the Bible. St. Paul indicated the spiritual purpose of the link when he wrote, "So then, just as sin entered the world through one man and death through sin, so also death spread to all people because all sinned....For if the many died by the trespass of this one man, it is even more certain that God's grace, and the gift given by the grace of the one man Jesus Christ, overflowed to the many!" (Romans 5:12-15). Based on the information given in the various biblical genealogies, the age of the Earth since its creation appears to be about 6000 to 7000 years, although some would extend the upper limit to 10,000 or 12,000 years.[9]

Scientists have numerous ways of measuring the age of the Earth and the universe. We will consider those of physics here and those of cosmology later. Let us recall, as explained in chapter 3, that scientists can only measure an apparent age of anything based on their instruments and their methods. There is no way for them to validate their age estimate because time travel violates the known laws of physics. On the other hand, the apparent age as measured

---

[9] Partial genealogies exist in numerous of the historical books of the Old Testament where the lifespans of various kings and the ages at which they ascended to the throne are recorded. Longer genealogies are given in Genesis 5:3-32 and Genesis 11:10-26.

by the principles of physics is extremely well documented.[10] For example, if we look at all the isotopes that naturally occur on the Earth, we find that all the stable isotopes exist, and all the radioisotopes consistent with the Earth being more than a billion years old also exist. However, none of the additional radioactive isotopes that would be present if the Earth were less than a billion years old are present. Let us examine how this can be true. Consider radioactive isotopes A, B, and C, where A would decay to non-detectability in 1000 years, B in 10 million years, and C in 10 billion years. If the Earth were 10,000 years old, isotopes B and C would still be found, but isotope A would have decayed to non-detectability. However, if the Earth were one billion years old, only isotope C would still be found, because both isotopes A and B would have decayed to non-detectability. Based on the radioactive isotopes we do and do not find on Earth, the apparent age of the Earth must be between one and eleven billion years. This can be called Earth's "isotopic age." By dating individual rocks using method two as described above, a more refined age of about 4.6 billion years for the Earth has been calculated.

Is it possible new evidence might be found to change this estimate of the Earth's apparent age? Extremely unlikely. The dating process is based on well-understood fundamental physics of the atomic nucleus. The measurement methodology is simple and has been applied to this research area since the 1950's. Measurements are highly reproducible. Improvements in instrumenttation and methodology have only made the data more precise. Moreover, because all isotopes of a particular element are chemically the same, they all cluster together wherever the element is found. If the isotopes necessary to establish a younger age for the Earth existed, they would have been found everywhere any of the element was found.

As we saw in chapters 3 and 4, God gave the Earth an apparent age that is much older than its actual age when he created it because living plants needed a fertile soil and a developed atmosphere to survive. He did not tell us what that apparent age was. Our apologetic position must be that what God did tell us in Genesis 1 indicates he created the Earth with an apparent age that was significantly greater than its actual age. Therefore, we have no reason or basis to dispute with scientists what that apparent age is. The apparent age that God

---

[10] A detailed discussion of dating by radioactive elements is given in chapter 5 and appendix II of *Creating a Path for the Gospel*, pp. 110-114, 325-336.

gave the Earth and that has been measured by scientists does not impact our belief in what is revealed in Genesis 1. We need only point out why there is a difference between the actual age of the Earth and what scientists measure.

Cosmology – The Age of the Universe

Astronomy is an ancient science because the nighttime sky has been available everywhere for people to look up and wonder about.[11] The quality of the data, however, was not very good until the invention of the telescope at the beginning of the seventeenth century. Within the next hundred years the application of trigonometry and calculus to the stellar observations allowed astronomy to bloom. After Albert Einstein developed the theory of general relativity, physics began to be applied to astronomical data to create the field of astrophysics. This led to the field of cosmology, which attempts to explain the origin and the operation of the universe. Cosmology became well known after the formulation of the big bang theory, which unified the field in the same way that the plate tectonic theory unified geology (see next section).

Cosmology has only the data that the various branches of astronomy can collect. That data is gathered from viewing the whole electromagnetic spectrum coming from space, as well as from the rare neutrino bursts and from the gravitational waves that are large enough to be detectable on Earth. The development of special kinds of telescopes and the rapid improvement in measuring instrumentation have permitted scientists to collect and record monumental amounts of astronomical observations. The evidence gathered has allowed cosmologists to develop the big bang theory in incredible detail. They currently estimate that the universe is about 14 billion years old. Cosmology is inspiring to many people because they fantasize traveling around the universe. By the end of the twentieth century, a great interest in exoplanets[12] developed. Ingenious methods have been devised to study stars to seek such planets in the hope of finding intelligent life such as that which is dramatized in science fiction. Indeed, it appears that many stars do have planets.

Despite its popularity, cosmology has significant weaknesses as a science. First, it is completely observational. Due to the great distances in space, probes cannot be sent to what appear to be other stars and other galaxies. Exoplanets, which appear Earth-like from many lightyears away, might be more

---

[11] Filippenko, *Understanding the Universe*.
[12] An "exoplanet" is a planet orbiting a star other than the sun.

like the moon, Venus, or Mars than Earth on closer examination. The extreme physics that solutions to the general theory of relativity predict to be occurring in space cannot be duplicated here on Earth. The initial phases of the big bang are incomprehensible, and such physics have never actually been observed. As of this writing, dark matter and dark energy, which are postulated to make up 95% of the substance of the universe, have never been seen, although their effects have been detected. Finally, what is seen in the heavens is postulated to be a time-stratified view, with the light we see from some stars having left them only a few years ago, but the light from other features of the sky having left them 100 million or more years ago. Being a young science, cosmology is likely to see a lot of development.

From the viewpoint of the creation apologist, cosmology is still largely speculation because most of the light coming from space is a separate creation of God that did not actually come from stars. This idea was introduced in chapter 4 and is critical to our apologetic position. Light that we see from anything thought to be more than 6000 to 7000 lightyears away must have been created as light rays because the light from those objects themselves would not yet have had time since their creation to reach the Earth. Concerning these heavenly features, what we see is therefore created light and not stars and galaxies that may lie behind the light. Unlike the methods used in physics to date the Earth, where the objects being analyzed are real and can be measured in different ways, a substantial portion of the data used in cosmology could be only light rays, not radiated light. We have no experimental way to tell whether the bulk of the universe exists or is just God's special effects. This situation may seem outrageously weird, but it is true. Unless something can be brought into the laboratory or unless a laboratory can be sent to it, any model that fits what is observed from the Earth may be the correct explanation. This is the manner in which our eyes are fooled by the backdrops for sets in movies. That the Almighty God created only the light and not the stars fits the evidence, whether that model is correct or not. Because we cannot currently (and perhaps ever) send probes beyond the solar system, we cannot know how many of the "starry host" are real sun-like spheres and not merely part of God's cosmic backdrop for his earthly stage.

What is important here is not whether all or any of the stars exist. That is speculation because we cannot send probes thorough the universe to ascertain the actual situation. The important point is that God created light before it could have arrived from stars, due to the speed of light, based on what is revealed in Genesis 1:16. This means God has controlled what man has seen in the heavens since the fourth day, so we should not be too hasty in claiming we know what is in the heavens today.

Geology – The Structure of the Earth

Although God told us he created the various aspects of the surface of the Earth, he has given us very little detail about how and when he did such forming of surface features.[13] As previously mentioned, God can create objects out of nothing, or he can create them by rearranging what he had previously made. Were there nothing but surface features of the Earth to consider, we could easily accept that God created and shaped the Earth to his liking and leave the matter at that. However, people have discovered many things under the surface of the Earth. The ground has layers of different types of soil and rocks. There are fossilized bones and the impressions in rocks of plants and animals that do not exist on Earth today. There are minerals that can be smelted into metals and burnable substances like coal, oil, and natural gas. Our curiosity leads us to wonder how these things got into the ground. Because God did not tell us how these materials became buried in the Earth, we realize their existence and history are unimportant to our salvation. Nevertheless, their presence has spawned many theories and has been used to attack the Genesis creation account, so we need to consider them.

Geology is a much newer science than chemistry or physics, so it was not until well into the twentieth century that the field of geology developed a unifying theory for what has been observed on the Earth.[14] Before that happened, it was easy for Christians to try to "debunk" the evidence of those advocating evolutionary explanations for the development of the Earth's surface. Older books by Christians referred to artifacts that had been discovered that seemed to disprove geological claims. They offered counter-theories explaining that what could be observed was a result of the great flood at the time of Noah. However, by the middle 1960's a model called the "plate tectonic theory" gained general acceptance by geologists. It has since been strengthened great-

---

[13] "For the LORD is the great God and the great King above all gods. He holds the unexplored places of the earth in his hand, and the peaks of the mountains belong to him. The sea belongs to him, for he made it, and his hands formed the dry land" (Psalm 95:3–5).

[14] Renton, *The Nature of Earth*.

ly by extensive evidence that have been collected, frequently using automated sensors, from every portion of the Earth.

The basic idea upon which plate tectonics was developed is that the Earth's surface, both its land and its sea, are resting on dozens of plates of various sizes. These plates slowly slide past each other, collide with each other to form mountain ranges, part from each other to form troughs in the sea, and sometimes slide under other plates. Thanks to ultrasensitive detection equipment, the relative movements of points on the Earth's surface has been confirmed. The edges of the plates and the plates' speed and direction of motion have been mapped in great detail. It is postulated that as the plates interact, they scrape material from each other, much as when two automobiles sideswipe. The vast improvements in our ability to do analysis of trace minerals and metals allegedly transferred in such collisions have permitted the development of a model that details the supposed history of these collisions over a period of hundreds of millions of years. Trace mineral analysis, like DNA analysis, has greatly strengthened the ability to do falsification challenges in geology. It is no longer possible for someone to propose a new model of how a valley or a mountain was formed or of how sea levels changed without showing how the new model accounts for all the trace minerals and other transferred substances that can be measured.

Prior to the development of the tectonic plate model, geologists were justly criticized for using unreliable dating methods and theories of mass transport that were often heavily based on supposition. As a result of this new model and of greatly improved analytical methods that geology imported from chemistry and physics, geology has dramatically improved its reputation as a science that constructs well-documented models. Two limitations continue to exist in geology, however. First, geologists must sometimes use less reliable dating methods, involving rock-wasting, sedimentation rates, and embedded fossils, although not as extensively as in the past. Second, geology is primarily an observational science, where experimentation cannot be performed on large-scale processes. Rather, these processes must be extrapolated from observation of and experimentation with small-scale processes.

Paleontology – The Development of Life

If it were not for the fossils embedded in rock formations, we could treat the claims of geologists as we do the apparent age of the Earth, namely, as artifacts of the way in which the LORD created the world to be his stage for mankind. Because fossils do exist, we need to extend our discussion into the domain of paleontology. Paleontologists study fossils to build maps of how species supposedly evolved from one-celled organisms to the creatures that we encounter today, including man. When the fossils are thought to be of human origin, then a separate field of study called "anthropology" becomes involved, but the techniques are similar. Paleontologists do have a large amount of quality evidence, and they work with geologists to place their evidence onto the geological calendar of the events that happened on Earth. There is a real symbiotic relationship between these disciplines because each group helps the other assign dates to its evidence. If life had evolved on the Earth, then the work of the paleontologists and anthropologists would be critical to the work of the evolutionary biologists who are trying to determine how that evolution happened. (We will consider this in the next section.) It is natural for scientists, driven by their fundamental assumption, to assume evolution is the cause of the fossils.

How does the creation apologist respond to the dual challenge of geology and paleontology? First, we must admit we cannot know how or when God buried the fossils because the Bible does not mention fossils. God could have done this any time from when he created the world until the time people began searching for them. Second, we cannot know whether all the fossils are the remains of real plants, animals, and anthropoids that lived or whether some or all of them are created artifacts placed in the ground as a test of our faith. Concerning this possibility Moses warned the Israelites, "If a prophet or an interpreter of dreams arises among you, and he predicts a sign or wonder for you, and the sign or wonder that he promised you comes true, and he says, 'Let's go after other gods that you do not know, and let's serve them,' do not listen to the words of that prophet or that interpreter of dreams, because the LORD your God is testing you to see whether you really love the LORD your God with all your heart and with all your soul" (Deuteronomy 13:1–3). God could have done numerous unknown things with the plants and animals he created that we cannot imagine in his process of creating the world and modi-

Creation Apologetics 143

fying it into the form in which we see it today.[15] The apologist's best answer is that God has placed in the ground of the Earth what he knew would be best for his purposes. He has not asked us to explain what he did, nor has he given us the ability to make such explanations. He has told us all things exist through his creative action[16] and has instructed us to believe what he has revealed.[17] If someone ridicules us for ducking the question by playing the "God card," then our response should be that we must play the hand God has dealt us and not try to pull cards out of our sleeves. It is a matter of faith in God's revelation.

Biology – The Origin of Life

Perhaps no subject has been more vigorously disputed between believers in creation and believers in evolution than how life originated on Earth.[18] The Bible clearly states that God created the universe out of nothing on the first day (Genesis 1:1) but that he can also create things out of preexisting matter as he did in the rest of Genesis 1. Mankind is limited to creating things out of preexisting matter. We take for granted people can create buildings out of various materials—some from materials that once were living, such as wooden houses, and some from inanimate materials, such as adobe houses. Mankind can also mimic God's creating activities by making artificial diamonds and by changing the locations of land and water through building levees, canals, dams, and artificial lakes. This situation leads to two critical questions: "Could man create life?" and "Could life evolve spontaneously?"

The first question needs some clarification. People have long bred plants and animals to create new generations that have distinctive characteristics. They have even bred animals across species, such as donkeys with horses to

---

[15] We are tempted to let our imaginations run wild and envision numerous scenarios through which God could have manipulated the earth in order to explain all the evidence that geologists and paleontologists have found up to this time. These scenarios, however, would be based on speculation and not on revelation, so they would prove nothing and only divert our hearts from relying on what has been revealed.
[16] [God said,] "For in six days the LORD made the heavens and the earth, the sea, and everything that is in them, but he rested on the seventh day." (Exodus 20:11)
[17] [Moses wrote that God acted,] "In order to teach you that man does not live by bread alone, but man lives by every word that comes from the mouth of the LORD." (Deuteronomy 8:3)
[18] Steven Nowiscki, *Biology: The Science of Life*, The Great Courses (Chantilly, Virginia: The Teaching Company, 2010).

create mules. Is this creating life? Since scientists in the latter part of the twentieth century developed the technology to sequence the DNA of plants and animals, they have been able to isolate genes from one species and move them into another species. For example, bacteria have been created by gene-splicing that can produce human insulin, and some crops have, in the same manner, been made more resistant to unfavorable soil conditions, blight, and pests. These examples produced new species that transmit the characteristics introduced into them to future generations. Is this creating life? Further research is being done to improve the genes themselves. In fact, this might become a major research area in the future. Would this be creating life? Finally, using our current technical knowledge, it would be possible to create a process to synthetically produce a living DNA molecule from inorganic compounds, even though the process would be tedious and of little practical value.[19] Would this be creating life?

Scientists have demonstrably acquired the technology to create life and to restructure how living organisms function. The accomplishments of man in developing this ability should not raise biblical issues for the apologist. Genesis is clear in its declaration that God originally created life on earth from the non-living materials already present. The Bible, however, never states that man could not also create other life forms through his own processes. In fact, the LORD did not restrict man when he gave him "dominion over the fish of the sea, and over the birds of the sky, and over the livestock, and over all the earth, and over every creeping thing that crawls on the earth" (Genesis 1:26). God, however, gave clear warnings that man himself is special and that he is not to change the nature of his own being. That is, in reality, what Eve tried to do in Genesis 3. The Bible documents the special status of man in Genesis 1:27, saying, "God created the man in his own image" and in Genesis 2:7, saying, God "breathed into his nostrils the breath of life." In Genesis 9:5, God said, "In fact, I will hold each animal and each person responsible for your lifeblood." God will hold man responsible for any evil he does to his fellowmen, whether someone uses a club or genetic engineering to try to reshape their substance.

The second question is totally different. Based on the fundamental assumption of science, scientists must conclude that life evolved spontaneously. Eve-

---

[19] Because whole genes can readily be cut out of DNA molecules and used for further molecular synthesis, the synthesis of DNA from its chemical elements would merely be an academic exercise.

ryone agrees the process would have been incredibly complex and improbable, yet researchers in the life science generally believe it happened. Evolutionary biologists, therefore, need to establish a feasible path through a labyrinth of problems and to prove each necessary step is feasible and could be succeeded by the next step in the process in a natural environment. The findings of paleontology are used to guide some of this work. Many researchers are working on the numerous aspects of this problem, but the progress is, not unexpectedly, slow.

The creation apologetic position here is extremely strong. First, scientists need to demonstrate the whole process before they can convincingly argue it could have happened. Until that occurs, the apologist need do nothing except to point out the burden of proof is on the proponents of the evolutionary model. We are not obligated to prove something cannot happen. Second, even if after enormous effort the proponents could show a complex pathway does exist that could have produced life spontaneously, it would not mean such spontaneous generation did occur. This is an example of the affirming-the-consequent fallacy with which all inductive reasoning is burdened. Just because something could have happened in a certain way does not mean it did happen in that way. The apologist can continue to point to the biblical explanation of the actions of the almighty God as a viable alternative to any convoluted natural process.

Archeology – The Origin of Human Culture

Numerous artifacts of human civilization have been found buried in the ground.[20] Archaeologists have used these to study the movements and cultural development of peoples across the face of the Earth. Their efforts to date human civilizations have produced timelines that are much longer than are compatible with the genealogical information given in the Bible. Some of these timelines run back tens of thousands of years. How does the creation apologist handle such claims by archeologists?

Archeology is an observational science. Archeologists are limited by what they happen to find. To preserve sites for future work, they strictly limit how much of the sites they excavate. If their excavations are dated within the last

---

[20] Eggert and Kieta, *Clearing a Path*, pp. 193-223.

five thousand years, there is little that a creation apologist would find of concern. It is archeologists' efforts to push thousands of years further into the past where conflict is certain to arise. The further back they go, the more archeologists need to rely on carbon-14 for dating; however, it is precisely in this era that the carbon-14's concentration in the atmosphere might have been significantly different. There is also the matter of whether all the materials at a particular site came from the same era and therefore can be associated with and used to date other items. For example, good campsites might have been used frequently over millennia, and advanced tools, through trade and theft, might have moved long distances from where they were created. Could some ancient archeological sites be pre-flood and others post-flood? God has told us almost nothing about the people living before the flood. On the other hand, God has caused a tremendous diversity of features to occur in people and in animals since the time of the flood. Did God's changes materially affect what archeologists and anthropologists find in their various digs? Only he knows.

The apologist must recognize the severe limitations that archeologists face when they study sites from an era when there were no written records and no calendars. Cuneiform, the oldest writing form, dates to 3400 BC. The Maya calendar begins in 3114 BC, although its development may have been more recent. These first instances of human recordkeeping are not that far in the past. Without firm anchor points and with a questionable primary measuring tool for time, dating more ancient archeological sites is highly speculative, and we should treat all claims with deep skepticism. The almighty God's ability to alter the carbon-14 content of the atmosphere, as well as other anchor points used for dating, can make the apparent dates on a timeline much different than the actual dates. As apologists, we can point out that if God altered the Earth's environment, archeological timelines are unreliable. Once again, the lack of a time machine prevents scientists from refuting our position.

Summary of Apologetic Approaches

We can see three distinctly different approaches that the apologist can use, depending on the nature of the science and its development. In some cases, we can accept what scientists have learned because it does not challenge biblical revelation. For example, Genesis 1 gives us information about creation that indicates God created entities with an apparent age; therefore, we can easily explain why scientists might find an apparent age of the Earth much older than its actual age. The creation of new forms of life in the laboratory is

Creation Apologetics

in line with God giving man dominion over the other life forms. Apologists need not defend against claims that can be easily reconciled with the Scriptures.[21] We should not look for disputes.

Second, some models, such as those from geology and paleontology, are consistent with the evidence that can be found, but that evidence is not inconsistent with the Bible because the Bible makes no mention of what these fields are studying. Simply because evidence is consistent with a scientific model does not prove that the model is correct. The logical fallacy of affirming the consequent prevents this. God created fossils and the tectonic plates and put them where we find them for reasons of which we who rely on divine revelation are unaware. We believe God had his reasons, as he has for everything he does, but he did not share them with us. Scientists may regard certain evidence as being of great importance for their evolutionary models, but if the evidence itself does not directly contradict what is written in the Bible and if creating it is not outside the scope of what God might do, then we should not feel threatened by such evidence. We simply reply we do not know why it exists, but we will ask God when we see him in heaven.

A third apologetic approach is to present the biblical position as divinely revealed and challenge our opponents to present evidence meeting best scientific practices to disprove it. This approach puts the burden of proof on the opponents. For example, in cosmology it is impossible to experimentally probe the universe on which cosmological theories are built. Similarly, demonstrating a path of reaction steps between the chemical elements and advanced life forms in an environment that would permit all the steps to occur in sequence without human intervention will be an incredibly difficult task. We are under no obligation to defend against such speculation. We do not need to do anything before cosmologists and evolutionary biologists can demonstrate in the laboratory that their models are feasible. It would be foolish to allow ourselves to transfer the burden of proof from them to us. Even if evolutionists succeed in demonstrating some major claim, they still have not shown that God did things the way they propose.

---

[21] We need to recall how falsely reading the geocentric universe into the fourth day of creation led the Roman Catholic Church to persecute astronomers who proposed the heliocentric model, even when they backed their claims with solid evidence.

As believers in the Almighty LORD who created the universe out of nothing and has managed it using both his natural and supernatural hands, we are in an invincible position. Who can challenge whether an omnipotent God could create the world as we see it today? "For he [God] said, 'Let it be,' and it was! He gave a command, and there it stood" (Psalm 33:9). Whatever we see in the heavens, find on the earth, or discover in the laboratory can easily be explained in terms of God's will and his power. Then too, who can cure the inherent weaknesses of inductive reasoning that scientists are forced to use and that make all their models provisional, forever prisoners to the next piece of evidence that is discovered? We can only put ourselves at a disadvantage if we try to develop and defend our own explanations of how things happened by the laws of nature. What happens when we do that is the subject of the final chapter.

13

Flawed Apologetic Approaches

Apologetics is not about protecting God or his reputation. What can puny humans do to protect the omnipotent God? It would be like a troop of cub scouts armed with plastic bats trying to protect a brigade of the army's latest battle tanks. Yet humans are always tempted to show their "superior" intelligence by coming to the rescue of God when he seems to falter or become a bit doddery. In the last chapter we tried to avoid this by showing that many things from science do not challenge God's Word at all, if we stop trying to read our ideas into it, and other things God has handled in his own way, even if he has not told us about it. We only need to challenge scientists when they make claims that cannot be validated through best practices and therefore are necessarily only speculative.

Many would-be apologists want to go further. Either they want to trim the message of God's Word to make it agree with the "discoveries" of science, they want to disprove science, or they want to develop their own science by restricting God's actions. All such approaches are logically flawed and theologically dishonest because they try to dictate to God how he must have behaved. Worse yet, they are useless in preserving faith because only the Holy Spirit can do that, and he only works through the means of grace, namely God's Word and the sacraments. We will consider some popular approaches for "aiding God" and why they are ineffective even if scientifically uneducated people can be led to believe them.

Theistic Evolution

Historically, universities contained faculties in areas such as religion, law, medicine, mathematics, and science. Scholars often crossed over from one discipline to another, and they regarded themselves as one community attemptting to learn a unified truth. That common fabric of thought began to unravel when scientific research produced evidence seemingly incompatible with the revelation given in the Bible. This situation led to efforts to reconcile teachings about God with the growing amount of evidence that seemed to indicate biological evolution had occurred. Those involved embraced a general evolutionary view of the universe and rejected the idea of a special creation. They thought they could somehow harmonize evolutionary thought with a belief in God.

Already in the eighteenth century some scientists were questioning whether new species could arise. The discovery of fossils of extinct species in the nineteenth century, followed by Charles Darwin's work, led many to believe life had evolved. It was quickly recognized that such evolution would have taken a long period of time, meaning the biblical timeline was definitely too short. As scientists accumulated more and more evidence from various fields that was consistent with a much older Earth, theologians, many of whom had already embraced rationalism, saw the necessity of also accepting the new models of the Earth that were being developed. Their efforts resulted in what is now called "theistic evolution." The major tenets theistic evolutionists accept are 1) the prevailing cosmological model, 2) evolution and natural selection within species, 3) humans as a product of evolution, and 4) humans also having a spiritual nature. There is disagreement over whether God was the original creator of the materials of the big bang and over the extent to which he has intervened in the history of the universe, if at all, during its existence.

Theistic evolution is incompatible with the Christian faith, even if numerous mainline Protestant churches embrace it, and it is the doctrine of the Roman Catholic Church.[1] First, while some theistic evolutionists accept Genesis 1:1, all reject the rest of Genesis 1 and 2. But rejecting the revelation of God is to call God a liar. Samuel the prophet said, "The Splendor of Israel will not lie or change his mind, because he is not a man, who changes his mind" (1 Samuel 15:29). St. Paul stated his apostleship was "based on the hope of eternal life, which God, who cannot lie, promised before time began" (Titus 1:1,2). Jesus said to his heavenly Father in prayer, "Sanctify them by the truth. Your word is truth" (John 17:17). While theistic evolutionists might use the term "myth" rather than "lie" about the contents of Genesis, the meaning is the same. Yet, the account in Genesis 1 through 3 is narrative history, not po-

---

[1] *Catechism of the Catholic Church* (New York: Doubleday, 1994), pp. 83-84.

Flawed Apologetic Approaches

etic, and there is no indication in the text that it should be understood in any way other than as literal truth. If this account is not true, then God has intentionally misled us. That would make God a liar, and it would place him into the same category as Satan, whom Jesus called "the father of lying" (John 8:44).

Second, if the narrative text of Genesis 1 and 2 is not true, then the fundamental assumption of biblical Christianity that the Bible is the inerrant, verbally inspired Word of God is false. As we have seen, the creation account extends throughout the whole Scripture. The Bible would no longer be the source of divine revelation because none of the narrative text in any part of the Bible could be trusted to be true. One would have to "play God" and personally decide which, if any, parts of the Bible were true and which parts were false. This approach is in the realm of philosophy, not theology or science.

Third, if mankind evolved from other life forms, then it would be of like substance with them. Mankind would be just a stage in biological evolution and could not be held morally responsible by God. If that were true, a just God could not punish mankind for being yet inadequately developed, and no savior from sin would be necessary. In other words, no law implies no need for the gospel. Christianity as a religion would make utter nonsense. To argue mankind could have become moral would imply either that there was some type of break in the evolutionary process through which man became morally accountable or that any animal or plant might also be or could become a moral being. Without a special intervention in history by God, mankind could not have become different morally than any other species. Theistic evolutionists can document no such intervention, so their "god" is not the God of the Bible but an idol of their own making. Moreover, such a supernatural intervention would violate the fundamental assumption of science. Theistic evolution is incompatible with the worship of the LORD, the God of the Bible, and makes no sense to scientists.

Intelligent Design

The underlying premise of intelligent design is that the universe is so complex and so fine-tuned it could not have evolved naturally without the active guidance of some intelligent agent. This premise is often called the "teleological" argument for divine creation. Those making this assertion frequently use the eukaryotic cell,[2] which is the type of cell present in most living organisms, as their prime example of such incredible complexity. Certainly, eukaryotes are extremely complex, with structural, biochemical, signaling, and material transport properties that stagger the imagination. Many people regard the teleological argument as the strongest argument against large-scale evolution, often using an inappropriate understanding of entropy[3] to buttress their reasoning. Yet, as we explore this idea, it is essential we realize it arises from philosophical considerations. We must see whether there is scientific, logical, or theological justification supporting it.

Intelligent design, of course, violates the fundamental assumption of science and is therefore unacceptable to scientists. Let us examine why scientists are not as concerned with complexity as the non-scientists by considering the common snowflake. During winter storms, snowflakes with thousands of different patterns of six-fold symmetry fall in great numbers out of the chaotic environment of the clouds. In scientific words, clouds with high entropy produce snowflakes with low entropy. How can this be? How can such perfect order of so many different forms come out of such disorganization? The answer is that clouds are not closed systems, but exchange matter and energy with their surroundings; therefore, the concept of entropy cannot be directly applied. After studying the phenomenon, meteorologists have developed a general explanation for the formation of snowflakes, but the important point is that "nature" is capable of complex organization in an arena where we would hardly expect it to occur. Because of this, we cannot deny that natural processes can of themselves generate complexity; in fact, they often do. That such complexity can develop in a very short timeframe means that the development of much greater natural complexity in a much longer timeframe cannot automatically be dismissed. In other words, the logical argument in favor of intelligent design fails.

How complex we consider something to be is an example of a phenomenon called our "mental anchor point."[4] When we enter a store, we have a mental

---

[2] Nowicki, *Biology*, Lecture 3.
[3] "Entropy" is a measurement of randomness and defined by the Boltzmann equation as equal to the Boltzmann constant times the natural logarithm of the number of microstates within a system. According to the second law of thermodynamics, the entropy of a closed system, a system that does not exchange matter or energy with its surroundings, must always remain the same or increase in any reaction. Entropy is not a force, but a number calculated based on what happens when forces are applied. This calculation is not always easy to do.
[4] Ryan Hamilton, *How You Decide: The Science of Human Decision Making*, The Great Courses (Chantilly, Virginia: The Teaching Company, 2016).

anchor price for what we desire to buy. If the listed price is dramatically higher or lower than that anchor price, we are unlikely to buy, because we assume that we are being overcharged or that the merchandise is inferior. In the same way, we have anchor points for complexity. Our anchor point for the complexity in math problems depends on whether we struggle to add two-digit numbers on paper or can easily multiply four-digit numbers in our heads. The novice chess player and the grandmaster have radically different views of the complexity of a chess position. If an expert in microcircuit technology were to try to explain the functioning and construction of a smartphone of circa 2020 to a person in 1820, the latter would be certain the construction of such a device would be impossible. The complexity we see in a situation is dependent upon our experiences, not just the actual level of complexity that exists.

We can easily be misled when we lack information. A magician can bedazzle us if we do not know how he does his tricks. While we can readily learn the methods of the sleight-of-hand artist, learning the methods that occur in nature, from the commonplace to the bizarre, takes a substantial amount of disciplined study. Almost everyone is exposed in high school, if not before, to the principles of Newtonian physics and to the Bohr model of the atom. These, however, are simplistic models of how nature really works. To a large extent, natural processes are governed by non-linear differential equations and by properties peculiar to specific substances for which the non-expert has no anchor points for guidance. Due to this, our reason and our sense of complexity are useless as guides to whether something can or cannot naturally occur. "I-science," in which the human mind tries to find scientific truth by reasoning, is no more reliable than "I-theology," in which the human mind tries to find theological truth by reasoning.

Furthermore, the philosophical argument for intelligent design cannot be converted into a scientific argument. To prove a complex substance, such as a eukaryotic cell, could arise naturally, scientists must perform the extremely difficult task of examining possible pathways until they find one, as was noted in chapter 12. The number of possibilities is astronomically large, but scientists can use the knowledge they acquire as they study the problem to concentrate their search on the most likely possibilities and give themselves a chance of success. On the other hand, to prove that some substance could not have come about naturally, the advocates of intelligent design would need to test absolutely all possible pathways. This is an incredibly more difficult task, and it is unclear how to make certain all possibilities would be examined and eliminated. Because of this, intelligent design advocates will never be able to produce valid verifiable evidence to disprove evolution. It is the difference between trying to find a lost baseball in a house and trying to prove a baseball is not in the house.

If we accept the fundamental assumption of biblical theology, then we will believe God created the world in six terrestrial days. Whether the world is too complex to have evolved by itself is consequently irrelevant. It is merely a distraction from Christ's Great Commission to the church. At this point some might object and quote, "The heavens tell about the glory of God. The expanse of the sky proclaims the work of his hands. Day after day they pour out speech. Night after night they display knowledge. They do not speak. They say no words. Their voice is not heard. Their voice goes out into all the earth, and their word reaches the end of the world" (Psalm 19:1-4) and "For every house is built by someone, and God is the one who built everything" (Hebrews 3:4). While these statements are true for Christians who accept the Bible as their standard of truth, they are not true scientifically and are open to challenge philosophically. The first nine chapters of this book present a much stronger case for God's creating activity than these two verses in isolation because these verses do not set a timeline or relate the creation to God's special creature man.

Because intelligent design is not restricted by the fundamental assumption of biblical Christianity, it can readily be used to justify a timeline for creation much longer than is compatible with biblical revelation. In attempting to establish the need for an "intelligent designer," i.e., a "god," intelligent design advocates have weakened the certainty expressed in the Bible. The LORD is not *per se* interested in our belief in a "creator god." He rather demands we believe everything he has revealed. Jesus answered the devil by quoting the word of God through Moses, "It is written: Man shall not live by bread alone, but by every word that comes out of the mouth of God" (Matthew 4:4). No person will be saved merely because he or she believes the world was created by a divine being. Creation is only one part of the plan involving God's relationship with mankind that the LORD decreed in eternity, as discussed in chapter 2. It is important, but it is not the central message of the Scriptures. We should not permit intelligent design to draw us into a let's-you-and-him fight scenario. If we accept its argument on complexity, we are forced to draw a line in the sand and say, "Science can never cross this line." What if science

Flawed Apologetic Approaches 155

does cross it, as it has crossed so many previous lines? We have nothing to gain and everything to lose by taking such a stand. The Bible does not require this of us, so why should we do it?

Creation Museums

Most people misunderstand the nature of museums.[5] All museums are businesses that need money to survive. That money comes from visitors and donors. The practices of a museum are driven by what it must to do to raise the money it needs to stay in business. Every year museums that fail to generate sufficient revenue collapse. While few museum operators are as crass as P. T. Barnum[6] in their business practices, the need for revenue often overshadows their commitment to accuracy.

Moreover, museums are established to influence people to adopt the museum founders' worldview on some theme, whether that theme is Abraham Lincoln or space aliens. Museum curators gather what materials they can for public display to support that worldview. Museum boards work to create a feeling of confidence, pride, reassurance, enthusiasm, commitment, or outrage, as appropriate, in museum visitors to get them to return and bring others. Museum administrators know people are not only curious but are also easily manipulated when their feelings are involved. Docents, whether museum staff members or volunteers, are trained to present the museum's message and seldom personally have expert knowledge. Therefore, it is prudent for museum visitors to regard any museum's displayed materials as not necessarily an accurate representation of all that is known about the theme of the museum. A city museum, for example, is likely to omit materials that would embarrass prominent families in the community. Museums can be educational, but visitors must not be overawed by what they see.

Creation museums cater to those who desperately want to see tangible evidence to validate their belief in creation. Such people generally have a poor understanding of either science or theology and have little ability to judge the

---

[5] The author of this book is a life member and former officer of the operating division of a railroad museum.
[6] Phineas Taylor Barnum was a nineteenth century American showman, businessman, and politician, remembered for promoting celebrated hoaxes, who supposedly said, "There's a sucker born every minute."

accuracy of what is presented to them. These museums therefore give Christians a false sense of security, encouraging them to rely on the works of man rather than on the Word of God for their faith.

Creation Science

The name "creation science" is an oxymoron. Divine "creation" is a concept that comes from the fundamental assumption of biblical Christianity, and "science" is defined by its own fundamental assumption. As we saw in chapter 11, these are incompatible assumptions. Despite this, the advocates of creation science try to use science to support creation.

Creation science involves two strategies. The first is to find evidence disproving or casting doubt upon an evolutionary theory in some branch of science. If creation science investigators follow the rules for collecting evidence and if they share that evidence with the scientific community, researchers in established scientific fields are delighted with their work. Unfortunately, it is common for evidence collected by creation science workers to fail to meet the accepted standards for scientific evidence. Most of their evidence is never shared with the scientific community. Instead, the evidence is presented to the scientifically untrained public, often with claims that have not been verified by a falsification challenge. The scientific community regards such activity as dishonest, as when cigarette companies used to hire PhD scientists to produce evidence showing cigarette-smoking did not cause cancer.[7] Being associated with perceived dishonesty weakens the ability of Christians to share the message of the gospel.

An even more insidious problem with this approach is that it is self-defeating. If the evidence discovered is irrelevant to the validity of the theory being challenged, it is a waste of resources and sometimes deceitful. If it does show weaknesses in a theory, then scientists will work to correct those weaknesses, making the theory even harder to challenge. In fact, this is what the

---

[7] In the 1960's researchers for the National Institute of Health amassed a large body of evidence showing that cigarette smoking was a major cause of cancer. Tobacco companies hired scientists who began "finding" evidence showing that cigarette smoking was safe and even healthy. This created an emotional justification that permitted many smokers to continue smoking. The experiments conducted by the tobacco company scientists, however, were set up in a biased manner to produce results that favored the industry's claims. Even worse, those results that were unfavorable were never released to the public but were kept locked in company safes. Other companies have similarly falsified experiments and hidden unfavorable evidence, which is why there are federal agencies that monitor certain corporate research.

Flawed Apologetic Approaches

scientific community does all the time. Challenging and amending theories is their bread and butter. Because of this, negative scientific evidence quickly loses its relevancy at the cutting edge of scientific research. Once a theory is adapted to account for legitimate contrary evidence, that evidence is outdated because it no longer points to a defect in the theory. As time passes, printed creation science materials become filled with claims about issues that have subsequently been resolved. Unless one is intimately familiar with the status of research in a field, one does not know which questions are still unresolved because the scientific community has not yet found satisfactory answers for them. There is an old saying in science, "If the ink on it is dry, the publication is out-of-date." Arguments based on out-of-date ideas hamper the Christian's ability to witness to the gospel. Thus, the first method of creation science is a lose-lose proposition for Christians. It either strengthens evolutionary models or it weakens our credibility.

The second approach used by creation science advocates is to develop their own theories to explain what is observed in nature. While this approach might, at first, sound promising, it forces creation science to make an unscriptural assumption. Let us consider the situation that scientists and creation science advocates both face. If an event is observed, such as an apple falling from a tree, it could have one of two causes: 1) The event could have occurred by the laws of nature that God created (i.e., by God's natural hand). 2) The event could have occurred either in whole or in part by the direct intervention of God in nature (i.e., by God's supernatural hand). As we saw in chapter 11, the fundamental assumption of science was made so scientists could rule out possibility 2. If a divine being occasionally caused some events to happen in the physical world, scientists could never be certain if what was observed was the result of the laws of nature or of divine intervention.

Those who believe in biblical Christianity must face this same issue, namely, how do we know whether God acted with his natural hand or whether he acted with his supernatural hand? The Bible tells us we cannot know this. St. Paul wrote, "For who has known the mind of the Lord, or who has been his adviser?" (Romans 11:34). We cannot know what the LORD plans to do or how he plans to do it. That was also true of things in the past, unless he has specifically told us. How he did and does things is part of the hidden knowledge of God. Isaiah wrote, "For the LORD of Armies has made plans, and who can stop him? His hand is stretched out, and who can turn it back?" (Isaiah 14:27). A psalmist wrote, "The LORD does whatever he pleases in the heavens and on the earth, in the seas and in all the depths" (Psalm 135:6). God himself said, "Indeed, from the first day, I am he. There is no one who can deliver anyone from my hand. I act, and who can reverse it?" (Isaiah 43:13). God has emphatically declared his independence of action. Therefore, Christians do not know how any event in this world occurs unless God tells us! We must "fear, love, and trust in God above all things," as Luther taught in his explanation of the First Commandment, and that includes "above" our understanding of nature. Certainly, God allows us to build models of nature so that we can live our lives, but not so that we can bind him with our reasoning.

Creation science advocates ignore what God clearly declared to enable themselves to build their models. They assume God practices what has been called a "conservation of miracles." In other words, they claim that unless God indicated he worked through his supernatural hand, the great changes that have occurred on the Earth since the creation were done by God's natural hand, namely, the laws of nature. However, the concept of the conservation of miracles, no matter in what words it is expressed, is unscriptural. It places a limitation on how God works that he has not placed on himself.[8]

This is a troubling matter. Moses relayed the words of the LORD to the Israelites when he wrote, "Do not add to the word that I am commanding you, and do not subtract from it" (Deuteronomy 4:2). Whenever an unscriptural principle is used to attempt to clarify or to buttress our understanding of the Scriptures, our doctrine becomes corrupted. For example, John Calvin's thesis that "the finite cannot contain the infinite"[9] corrupted the doctrine of Christ among Calvin's followers. In another example, the thesis that we were elected "in view of faith" rather than "into faith" led the Lutheran churches accepting this thesis to slide ever deeper into theological error. God has not called us to be clever but to be faithful. St. Paul warned us, "See to it that no one takes you captive through philosophy and empty deceit, which are in accord with human tradition, namely, the basic principles of the world, but not in accord with Christ" (Colossians 2:8). No human tradition is more ingrained in us than

---

[8] References to God acting through natural or supernature means are only used for our benefit. From God's viewpoint all his actions are uniformly supernatural, but he often tailors them to our understanding of natural processes.

[9] Calvin claimed that the attributes of the infinite Son of God could not be contained in the finite body of Jesus, so the two natures of Christ were bounded together in the same manner as two boards might be glued together. The physical nature could only be present locally, while the divine nature could be omnipresent in the universe.

Flawed Apologetic Approaches 159

that we need to be able to explain everything, even when God has not given us the explanation.

From the viewpoint of the scientific community, advocates of creation science simply do not play according to the rules. First, any "scientific" model needs to take all the relevant evidence into consideration. Few among the proponents of creation science have sufficient scientific training to do this. Second, legitimate scientists always submit their theories to the scientific community as part of a falsification challenge. Those engaged in creation science rarely are willing to undergo such challenges. Instead, they place their ideas in front of those who will accept them unquestioningly as confirmation of their own preconceived notions. This practice leads people away from a trust in God to a trust in the works of man.

The world of science has radically changed since the 1970's. Up until that time, it was possible for fundamental scientific discoveries to be made by relatively unknown people working with limited financial resources. Since the Soviet launching of Sputnik in 1957, the governments of large industrial nations and many major companies have poured so much money into organized research that those without that type of backing cannot compete. Scientific evidence is being gathered, sorted, and archived in amounts and at speeds even the best scientists of previous eras could never have imagined. Without access to this data and the supercomputers to process it, those out of the loop, such as those trying to develop creation science models, have little chance of proposing anything that cannot readily be disproved or that has not been previously considered. Even the well-funded traditional scientific community sometimes needs to scramble to keep the numerous basic science models of the laws of nature synchronized across disciplines.

Jesus' parable about the two men who built houses, one on a rock and the other on sand,[10] is relevant to any effort to defend and explain divine creation using human methods, whether those methods be philosophical reasoning or alternate science. Scripture is a rock that does not change and was given by

---

[10] [Jesus said,] "Everyone who hears these words of mine and does them will be like a wise man who built his house on bedrock. The rain came down, the rivers rose, and the winds blew and beat against that house. But it did not fall, because it was founded on bedrock. Everyone who hears these words of mine but does not do them will be like a foolish man who built his house on sand. The rain came down, the rivers rose, and the winds blew and beat against that house, and it fell—it was completely destroyed" (Matthew 7:24-27).

God. Science is even worse than sand; it is a quagmire of evidence and human assumptions concerning how to interpret it. Based on the history of science, we can say with certainty 1) over time the amount of evidence will increase, 2) the assumptions for interpreting it will change, and 3) whole lines of reasoning will be abandoned. Who would build a defensive position on such a shifting mass when an unmovable rock was available? Who would put even one pillar on such boggy ground when all pillars could be placed on the rock? The rock on which we may stand secure is already ours, but we shall never own the quagmire.

In our creation apologetics we need to follow Jesus' advice to "be as shrewd as snakes and as innocent as doves" (Matthew 10:16). We must rely on the Holy Spirit to change hearts when we proclaim the whole counsel of the Scriptures rather than on our own shrewdness to change minds when we advance human arguments. Human arguments and evidence, no matter how well they are presented, cannot aid the Holy Spirit in his work. Building people's confidence in the LORD through the faithful teaching of his Word should be our goal rather than building a false confidence in quasi-scientific arguments that may collapse when people most need them. Rather than deceiving ourselves and then deceiving others, we need to restrain our longings to outsmart our opponents and instead rely on our God. Levitical singers known as the sons of Korah quoted the LORD, "Be still, and know that I am God. I will be exalted among the nations. I will be exalted on the earth" (Psalm 46:10). We need to tell our reason to be still and to trust our God to accomplish his will through his means.

Conclusion

In the preceding pages we have seen the LORD, the God both omniscient and omnipotent, at work. He is the great Creator God. Already in eternity he planned his creation. He issued his decrees and then he carried them out in the space and time that he created. He called the substance of the world into existence and then shaped it to meet his goals. He gave it an apparent age so it would function properly. He created life, diversified it, and took care of it. He created mankind and dealt with people after they rebelled against their loving Father. He used his creative powers to carry out his plan of salvation for mankind. He has also warned us that creation will have an end.

Having seen God at work, we have also seen man at work. We have seen the confessors over the centuries affirm their belief in God as the Creator. We have seen why scientists view God's creation much differently than Bible-believing Christians. We have examined what we can say about the scientific models that challenge the divine revelation in the Scriptures. We have considered the dangers into which we enter when we try to use our reason to reconcile what we see in nature with what God reveals in his Word about his creation.

We see this world as in a darkened glass,[1] and our understanding of the things of God is feeble. We strut and fret our hour upon life's stage and then are seen no more.[2] Nevertheless, we must remain committed to what God has revealed and not second-guess him where he did not think it wise to give us more complete information. King David wrote, "For who is God besides the LORD? And who is the Rock except our God?" (Psalm 18:31). In his explanation of the First Commandment, Martin Luther wrote, "We should fear, love, and trust in God above all things." And if we trust in God, we must also trust in his Word. The writer to Hebrews expressed it best, "By faith we know that the universe was created by God's word, so that what is seen did not come from visible things" (Hebrews 11:3).

---

[1] 1 Corinthians 13:12.
[2] Paraphrase of Macbeth's soliloquy in Act 5, Scene 5 of William Shakespeare's *Macbeth*.

Bibliography

Balge, Richard D. *Trinity*. Milwaukee: Northwestern Publishing House, 2001.

Ahern, Kevin. *Biochemistry and Molecular Biology*. Chantilly, Virginia: The Teaching Company, 2019.

Brenner, John M. *Conversion*. Milwaukee: Northwestern Publishing House, 2000.

Carroll, Sean. *Mysteries of Modern Physics*: *Time*. Chantilly, Virginia: The Teaching Company, 2013.

Christian, David. *Big History: The Big Bang, Life on Earth, and the Rise of Humanity*. Chantilly, Virginia: The Teaching Company, 2008.

Eggert, Arthur A. and Kieta, Geoffrey A. *Clearing a Path for the Gospel*. Sun Prairie, Wisconsin: In Terra Pax Lutheran Publishing, 2019.

Eggert, Arthur A. *Simply Lutheran*. Milwaukee: Northwestern Publishing House, 2020.

Filippenko, Alex. *Understanding the Universe: Introduction to Astronomy*, 2nd ed. Chantilly, Virginia: The Teaching Company, 2007.

Graebner, A. L. *Outlines of Doctrinal Theology*. Saint Louis: Concordia Publishing House, 1910.

Hamilton, Ryan. *How You Decide: The Science of Human Decision Making*. Chantilly, Virginia: The Teaching Company, 2016.

Hazen, Robert M. *The Joy of Science*. Chantilly, Virginia: The Teaching Company, 2001.

Keller, Brian R. *Bible*. Milwaukee: Northwestern Publishing House, 2002.

Koehler, Edward W. A. *A Summary of Christian Doctrine*, 3rd, Brent W. Kuhlman, ed. Saint Louis: Concordia Publishing House, 2006.

Kuschel, Harlyn J. *Christ*. Milwaukee: Northwestern Publishing House, 2007.

Lange, Lyle W. *Sanctification*. Milwaukee: Northwestern Publishing House, 1999.

Lockman, Felix J. *Radio Astronomy: Observing the Invisible Universe*. Chantilly, Virginia: The Teaching Company, 2008.

Luchterhand, Lyle L. *Man*. Milwaukee: Northwestern Publishing House, 1998.

McCain, Paul T., ed. *Concordia: The Lutheran Confessions*, 2nd ed. St. Louis: Concordia Publishing House, 2006.

Molstad, John A. *Predestination*. Milwaukee: Northwestern Publishing House, 1997.

Mueller, Wayne D. *Justification*. Milwaukee: Northwestern Publishing House, 2002.

Nafzger, Samuel H., ed. *Confessing the Gospel*, Vol. 1. St. Louis: Concordia Publishing House, 2017.

Nass, Thomas P. *End Times*. Milwaukee: Northwestern Publishing House, 2011.

Nowiscki, Steven. *Biology: The Science of Life*. Chantilly, Virginia: The Teaching Company, 2010.

Paustian, Mark A. *More Prepared to Answer*. Milwaukee: Northwestern Publishing House, 2004.

Paustian, Mark A. *Prepared to Answer*. Milwaukee: Northwestern Publishing House, 2004.

Renton, John J. *The Nature of Earth: An Introduction to Geology*. Chantilly, Virginia: The Teaching Company, 2006.

Schlink, Edward. *Theology of the Lutheran Confessions*, Koehneke Paul F. and Bouman, Herbert J. A., trans. Philadelphia: Fortress Press, 1961.

Schumacher, Benjamin. *Black Holes, Tides, and Curved Spacetime: Understanding Gravity*. Chantilly, Virginia: The Teaching Company, 2013.

Snodgrass, Eric R. *The Science of Extreme Weather*. Chantilly, Virginia: The Teaching Company, 2016.

Strogatz, Steven. *Chaos*. Chantilly, Virginia: The Teaching Company, 2008.

Urone, Peter Paul and Hinrichs, Roger. *College Physics*. Houston: OpenStax, 2019.

Index

Aaron, 94
Abel, 99
Abraham, 92
adam, 63
Adam, 46, 63, 87, 98, 114
affirming the consequent, 147
age
   actual, 38, 43, 137, 146
   apparent, 37, 38, 39, 43, 135, 136, 137, 146, 161
   isotopic, 137
   of Earth, 136
   of universe, 138
anchor point, 152
angels, 67, 72, 89, 104
anthropology, 142
apologetics, 133, 149
Apostles, 59, 71, 84, 104
archeology, 145
Arian heresy, 109, 114
Aristotle, 126
ark, 76, 92
Ark of the Covenant, 94
astronomy, 45, 129, 138
astrophysics, 45, 138
atmosphere, 38, 48, 135, 146
Augsburg Confession, 114
   Apology to, 114
Babbage, Charles, 8
Babel, 77
bacteria, 40, 48
Barnum, P. T., 155
Barstow, Susie, 6
beginning, 23, 27, 28, 58, 60
Beyer, Christian, 115
big bang theory, 25, 138, 150

biology, 143
   evolutionary, 142, 145
blaming God, 88
Book of Concord, 107
burden of proof, 145, 147
butterfly, 46
calibration curve, 135
Calvin, John, 121, 158
Canaan, 92
canon, 121
captivity, 53, 55, 95
carbon dioxide, 38
carbon-14, 135, 146
carnivore, 76
Catechism
   Large, 112
   Small, 110
caterpillar, 46
chemistry, 128, 140
circumcision, 92, 97
complexity, 39, 123, 152
Confutation, 114
conservation of miracles, 158
Constantinople
   First Council of, 109
cosmology, 125, 138, 147
courtroom, 104
creation of
   animals, 47
   birds, 46
   man, 61, 62
   plants, 37
   sea creatures, 46
   woman, 65
creation science, 156

creed
  Apostles', 108, 110, 112
  Athanasian, 109
  Nicene, 109, 114
crucifixion, 97
Cuneiform, 146
Cyrus, 95
da Vinci, Leonardo, 8
dark energy, 139
dark matter, 139
Darwin, Charles, 150
David, 79, 94
day, 30
Day of the LORD, 101, 103
Dead Sea Scrolls, 121
death, 89
decree of
  creation, 20, 23, 61
  predestination, 21, 98
  redemption, 20, 98
demons, 89
Diet of Augsburg, 114
DNA, 48, 76, 92, 141, 144
double blind studies, 131
dragon, 89
earth, initial, 25
Eden, 64, 67, 91
Edison, Thomas, 7
Egypt, 93, 109
Einstein, Albert, 130, 138
election, 21
electron, delocalized, 125
element, 134
Elijah, 78, 96
Elisha, 78
entropy, 152
eternity, 15, 18, 23, 61, 90, 109, 116, 144, 154
eukaryotes, 152
Eve, 64, 65, 69, 87, 98
everlasting, 17

evolution, theistic, 149
ex nihilo, 24, 63, 73, 106
exodus, 77, 93
exoplanet, 138
expanse, 31, 41, 154
fallacy
  affirming the consequent, 130, 145
  false premise, 129
  hasty generalization, 130
falsification challenge, 123, 159
Fisher, John, 7
Flacius, Matthias, 116
Formula of Concord, 116
fossils, 141, 142, 147, 150
fundamental assumption
  of science, 122, 127, 152
  of theology, 121, 126, 154
Galileo, 126
genealogies, 136
gene-splicing, 144
geocentric, 42
geology, 140, 147
God
  being, 10
  immutability, 16
  internal acts, 18
  knowledge, 11
  name, 11
  nature, 9
  power, 13, 40, 71, 93, 105
  preparatory acts, 19
Godhead, 27, 58, 61, 109, 112
God-man, 97
Gospels, 57, 83
gravitational waves, 138
gravity, 7, 36
Gropius, Walter, 6
hands of God, 73
hares, 46
head knowledge, 99

heliocentric, 42
herbivore, 48, 62
heresies, 126
hermeneutics, 120, 123
image of God, 61, 64, 114
intelligent design, 151
inventions, human, 5
Isaac, 93
isotope, 134
Israel, 93
Jacob, 93
Joshua, 93
Judah, 93
Judgment Day, 103
kind, 37, 46, 47, 65
land, 36
lifespan, 6, 15, 92
light
   first, 26
   nature of, 29
   significance of, 27
lightyear, 136
logic, 73, 124
Lord's Prayer, 111, 113
Luther, Martin, 2, 110, 161
Lutheran Confessions, 107
marriage, 66, 71, 111, 115
Mars, 139
Maya calendar, 146
Melanchthon, Philipp, 114
Messiah, 83, 92, 94, 96, 102
Messianic promise, 89
microorganisms, 39, 72
moon, 41, 44, 45, 139
Moses, 78, 93, 142
mountain ranges, 141
museums, 155
mythology, 51, 150

neutrino, 44, 138
New Testament, 71, 102
Newton, Isaac, 51, 130, 153
Nicaea
   First Council of, 109
Noah, 76, 92, 140
nucleus, 134
objective justification, 98
omnipotent, 18, 51, 71, 78, 148, 161
omniscient, 20, 69, 87, 161
one flesh, 66
original sin, 114
OT History, 51, 69, 75
oxygen, 38
ozone layer, 39
paleontology, 142, 147
Pauling, Linus, 131
periodic table, 134
person of Christ, 125
pharmacology, 128
physics, 39, 125, 136, 140, 153
plate tectonics, 140
Preserver, 111, 114
priests, 94
Prophets, 55, 71, 81, 95
punishment for sin, 89
quatenus, 108
quia, 108
quid pro quo, 112
rabbits, 46
radiation
   nuclear, 134
   solar, 33, 38, 43, 48
radioisotope, 134
reason, 73, 96, 124, 153, 161
reasoning
   deductive, 124
   inductive, 122, 125, 129

Red Sea, 78
Revelation, 105
Roman Catholic, 108, 114, 150
rules of evidence, 123
sabbath, 30, 52
Samson, 78
Satan, 68, 87, 97, 151
science, 122
   hard, 128
   observational, 129, 141, 145
   soft, 128
scientific method, 123
scientists, 130
Scriptural principles, 3
seas, 36
second heaven, 17, 40
sedes doctrinae, 121
sedimentation rates, 141
seed, 89
serpent, 68, 88
shame, 67, 69
soil, 33, 37, 48, 90, 140
sola scriptura, 3, 107
Solomon, 80
Son of God, 96, 115
space, 16, 24, 96

spacetime, 16, 24
Sputnik, 159
standard, 120, 122
stars, 41, 44, 135, 139
sun, 41, 43, 45, 78
teleological argument, 151
the fall, 67, 87, 114
theology, 120
time, 16, 23, 24, 30
trace minerals, 141
Tree of Life, 64, 91
Tree of the Knowledge of Good
   and Evil, 64
Trinity, 18, 26, 61, 96, 109, 114
troughs, 141
truth
   scientific, 123
   theological, 123
uranium, 135
Venus, 38, 139
Virgin Mary, 96, 115
Wisdom Literature, 53, 70, 79
Wright, Frank Lloyd, 6
yom, 30
Zechariah, 96

www.ingramcontent.com/pod-product-compliance
Lightning Source LLC
Chambersburg PA
CBHW071714090426
42738CB00009B/1773